An Historical Outline
of
Architectural Science

SECOND EDITION

ARCHITECTURAL SCIENCE SERIES

Editor

HENRY J. COWAN
Professor of Architectural Science
University of Sydney

Previously published

Thermal Performance of Buildings
by J. F. VAN STRAATEN

Fundamental Foundations
by W. FISHER CASSIE

Models in Architecture
by H. J. COWAN, J. S. GERO, G. D. DING and R. W. MUNCEY

Principles of Natural Lighting
by J. A. LYNES

Electrical Services in Buildings
by P. JAY and J. HEMSLEY

Architectural Acoustics
by ANITA LAWRENCE

Fire and Buildings
by T. T. LIE

Psychology for Architects
by D. CANTER

Spatial Synthesis in Computer-Aided Building Design
edited by C. M. EASTMAN

Wind Loading on Buildings
by J. MACDONALD

Design of Building Frames
by J. S. GERO and H. J. COWAN

Building Services
by P. R. SMITH and W. G. JULIAN

Sound, Man and Building
by L. H. SCHAUDINISCHKY

Man, Climate and Architecture—2nd ed.
by B. GIVONI

Architectural Aerodynamics
by R. M. AYNSLEY, B. J. VICKERY and W. MELBOURNE

An Historical Outline

of

Architectural Science

by

HENRY J. COWAN

Professor of Architectural Science
University of Sydney

SECOND EDITION

APPLIED SCIENCE PUBLISHERS LTD

LONDON

APPLIED SCIENCE PUBLISHERS LTD
RIPPLE ROAD, BARKING, ESSEX, ENGLAND

First edition 1966

Second edition 1977

ISBN: 0 85334 725 5

WITH 69 ILLUSTRATIONS

Printed in Great Britain by Galliard (Printers) Ltd Great Yarmouth

To Elizabeth Proskauer

Preface to the Second Edition

This book has been completely re-written in the light of the historical research and the many innovations of the last decade. However, the general layout and most of the illustrations have been retained. Some material has been deleted in order to maintain the character of the book as an outline of the subject.

My thanks are due to Dr Valerie Havyatt, who checked the entire manuscript, to Mrs Hilda Mioche who typed it, to Mr John Dixon who did the photographic work and to Mr R. M. Aynsley, Professor J. S. Gero and Professor P. R. Smith for helpful suggestions.

Sydney   H.J.C.

Preface to the First Edition

Science and engineering are traditionally taught as a logical development from experimental data, without regard to the historical sequence of the solutions or the difficulties encountered in deriving them. Architecture, on the other hand, is taught largely by studying the work of great masters, and the sense of history is never absent from this treatment, even when the work is recent.

The difference reflects a wider distinction in the outlook of the scientist and the creative artist. Attempts to bridge the gap have not been lacking during the last thirty years. Many scientists have shown great interest in the history of their subject, and the discipline imposed on modern architecture by engineered structures has been explored by several eminent architects, engineers and art-historians. I have attempted to take the middle line by dealing only with those aspects of science and engineering which have influenced current architectural design, so that the historical emphasis is placed on the recent past.

This book started originally as a series of lectures delivered at the Massachusetts Institute of Technology in 1961 and at Cornell University in 1962, in each case to a mixed audience of architects and engineers. I am indebted to Professor Lawrence Anderson for the invitation to lecture at MIT, to Dean Burnham Kelly for the invitation to spend a semester at Cornell which afforded the leisure for editing the lectures with the help of their Rare Books Department, and to all those members of Cornell University who made my stay so pleasant and profitable.

When Sydney University instituted the Master of Building Science Degree Course for architects, engineers and building scientists in 1963, it was decided to include sixteen lectures on the history of building science, and I then expanded the material to its present form by including a survey of the scientific background to our current ideas on environmental design and on industrialised building.

While the book is primarily intended as a text for senior students,

I hope that the subject will interest some general readers and in token of this expectation I have included a glossary of technical terms.

Many thanks are due to Mrs Rita Arthurson, Mrs Marian Barber and Mrs Nance Liddy for typing the manuscript, to Mr Hans J. Milton, B.Arch., for preparing the drawings and to Mr John Dixon for the photographic work. Mr Dixon, our Chief Laboratory Technician, also made most of the models illustrated. I am greatly indebted to all those who have previously written on the subject; their names are listed in the bibliography. Illustrations and quotations have been acknowledged where they occur. Finally, I should like to express my appreciation to my colleagues, and to my past and present students for their helpful criticisms.

Sydney   H.J.C.

Contents

The Traditional Architectural Forms, and the Beginning of the Era of Scientific Structural Design

> If a contractor build a house for a man, and does not build it strong enough, and the house he build collapses and causes the death of the house owner, the contractor shall be put to death.
>
> *From the Code of King Hammurabi of Babylon, about* 1600 BC.

1.1. THE TWO REVOLUTIONS

Large structures can be built without mechanically based design rules. The Great Pyramid of Khafra at Gizeh, near Cairo, built about 2600 BC, had a height of 146 m (479 ft); this height was not surpassed by any building prior to the 20th century. The Pantheon, completed in Rome in the year AD 123, had a span of 43 m (141 ft); this is still considered a large span, and it was not surpassed until the second half of the 19th century.

We know nothing of the rules of structural design employed by the Ancient Egyptians, Babylonians and Greeks; however, some of the empirical rules used by the Ancient Romans for structural design have survived [11, 27 and 86]. All are geometric in character, that is, they may be expressed as rules of proportion or as geometric constructions. During the Renaissance there was a rapid multiplication of such rules, and measured drawings through the centuries have added to the number.

Some of the structural rules given by Vitruvius [11] may be of ancient origin, and this applies also to his aesthetic rules, derived from musical harmony (Section 6.7). Geometry remained the basis of both aesthetic and structural rules until the 18th century, and this is perhaps one reason why competently designed classical structures generally also had a pleasing appearance.

We have by no means abandoned structural design by specifying proportions. Every building by-law contains some rules for dimensioning structural members by proportions, because there is no

1

satisfactory statical design method, and some of these rules have been used for centuries.

The main weakness of empirical rules lies in their limited range of applicability, and in the difficulty of distinguishing those based on sound empiricism from others derived from old superstititions or from mistaken generalisations of features found in famous buildings. Although proportional rules no longer form the main basis for determining structural dimensions, few architects or engineers fail to inform themselves about previous work before embarking on the design of an unconventional structure.

The chief difficulty in a procedure based entirely on development from precedent is the verification of the new design. The pace of innovations is today too fast to make gradual adaptation from previous structures feasible. The public reacts more unfavourably than formerly to collapse or serious structural damage when the formwork is removed. We can no longer afford to build a substantial prototype structure, as was frequently done in previous centuries to test the design.

Statics is of comparatively recent origin. The lever principle was the only part of it known to the Ancient Greeks and the systematic study of the subject started only in the 16th century.

The first attempts to apply statics to structural design were made in the 17th century. However, traditional masonry structures are very complex, and even today we have difficulty in analysing some of them by means of statics. Thus geometric rules remained the basis of structural design for traditional architectural forms, and they were still used in the late 19th century.

In the 18th century the Industrial Revolution produced a need for a new type of building in which the new manufacturing operations could be housed. The buildings were commonly designed by the engineers who made the engines for the factories, and it was therefore natural that iron should be used to provide fireproof buildings. Since iron has good tensile strength, appreciable spans could be achieved without complicated vaulting, using simply supported iron beams. These beams can be analysed by means of statics with relative ease. Thus in the early 19th century factory buildings were to an increasing extent designed by the engineers who built factory machinery, using statical rather than geometric rules.

The ever-increasing trend towards structural design based on extensive numerical calculations has been mainly responsible for the growth of a separate profession whose practitioners have a basically different educational background from that of architects.

In the late 19th century the prevailing philosophy of architectural design tended to accentuate the differences in outlook between architectural and structural design which the intellectually differing problems of the two aspects encouraged. It was possible to place any desired form of ornamentation on any economically appropriate structure, and it was thus unnecessary to consider both aspects together.

The revolution in architectural thought during the 20th century has entirely altered this relationship. Only in comparatively simple or conventional buildings is it possible at the present time to consider the overall architectural concept without reference to the structure.

The change has been largely caused, and certainly strongly encouraged, by economic circumstances. Greatly improved living standards have increased the cost of labour to such an extent that many traditional methods of construction have completely vanished and have been replaced by processes more amenable to mechanisation. The virtual disappearance of elaborately carved natural stone as a structural material is aesthetically a great loss, but it was inevitable if one bears in mind that the mason had to form the shape by cutting small chips slowly from the solid block.

1.2. STRUCTURE IN THE ANCIENT WORLD

Only two major structural materials were available to the Ancient World, namely timber and natural or artificial stone. Timber has moderate strength in both tension and compression, but limited durability; no ancient and few medieval timber structures have survived to the present day. Natural stone, concrete and brick have generally good durability and high compressive strength, but their resistance to tension is poor; this deficiency is largely responsible for the limitation of span in masonry structures prior to the 18th century.

The simplest form of structure consists of a combination of beams and columns. The horizontal members are subject to bending which induces tensile stresses on the lower face, and this severely limits the span of unreinforced masonry structures, however carefully designed. Using sufficiently long and deep pieces of high-strength stone, moderate spans can be achieved, and large buildings can be constructed by using many columns to support the stone beams. Some very large structures have been built by these means, as for example Stonehenge in southern England, and the temples of Ancient Egypt.

The huge pieces of hard stone were very heavy, and their cutting and handling needed a great effort. From that point of view alone vaulting, which requires only relatively small pieces of stone, is far more efficient. The Egyptians transported the stone by water as far as possible. Erection at a great height was performed by building a ramp which was subsequently demolished. Remains of such ramps are still visible [22].

In Egyptian temples there is little evidence of structural design. In some beams the depth is actually greater than the span. In Greek architecture the stone is utilised more economically, but the interior space is dominated by the columns which, depending on one's point of view, form either an adornment or an obstruction.

The absence of large spans in Egyptian and Greek architecture may have been due to a lack of interest on the part of the early religions in interior spaces, due to the warm climate which encourages outdoor living, or it may have resulted from a lack of technical skill in building large spans.

All the great masonry spans prior to the invention of reinforcement in the 19th century were therefore bridged by means of vaulting.

Fig. 1.1. Cross section through the Pantheon, completed in Rome in AD 123 in the reign of the Emperor Hadrian. The dome is a hemisphere of diameter 43 m (141 ft), and another 43 m diameter hemisphere can be inscribed in the lower portion of the building, touching its floor. The dome was built of concrete using a natural cement obtained from the slopes of Mount Vesuvius. The concrete aggregate consisted in its lower portion of broken brick. Above that were alternate layers of broken brick and tufa (a porous volcanic rock). The upper part of the dome was built with alternate layers of tufa and pumice, the latter especially imported from Mount Vesuvius to reduce the weight of the concrete [115]. The illustration was made in the 16th century for Andrea Palladio, published in his *Four Books of Architecture*, and copied therefrom for Lord Burlington's edition of *Palladio* [15].

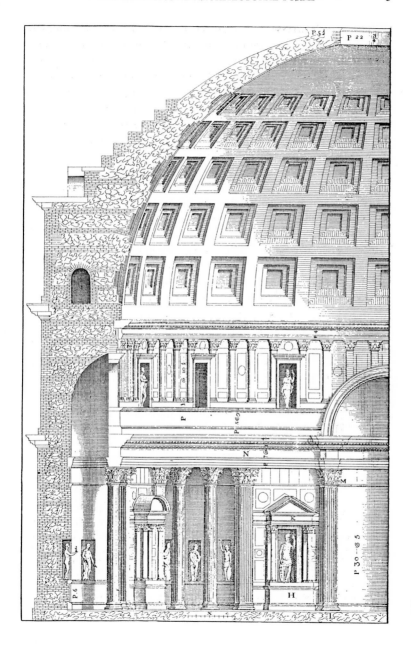

It seems likely that the arch developed from the use of corbels, *i.e.* stones cantilevered from the wall into the opening so that successive layers reduced the span.

The corbels are subject to tension on the upper face, but the span of the opening is reduced progressively by layers of stones or bricks, each layer cantilevering from the previous layer by only a short distance so that the tensile stresses are quite low.

In a true arch the stone is entirely in compression. Since the compressive strengths of stone, brick and concrete are about ten times their tensile strengths, the potential span is increased accordingly.

Both corbelled and true domes are of ancient origin. There is a corbelled space inside the Bent Pyramid, built about 2900 BC, and true arches of small span, which may date from 2500 BC, have also been found in Egypt. However, arches, vaults and domes never played an important part in Egyptian or Greek architecture; they were used only for buildings of minor significance.

The Roman contribution is therefore not the invention of the arch, but its utilisation for large spans. Some of the Roman arches, vaults and domes were of tremendous size, and their remains are still to be seen from Turkey to Spain and from Africa to Germany; Roman remains in Britain are on a smaller scale. The dome of the Pantheon (Fig. 1.1) has a span of 43 m (141 ft) which was not approached again until the 15th century (Section 1.5), and it was not surpassed in a building prior to the second half of the 19th century (Section 4.9).

Roman arches and domes were almost invariably circular. This may have been a matter of convenience in setting out the work; but it is more likely that the circle was used because it was regarded as the most perfect curve. When structural design was based on geometry, one would naturally assume that the geometrically perfect curve produced the strongest structure (Section 1.3).

Since the early 19th century (Section 1.5) we have known that the forces in a dome may be divided into two sets (Fig. 1.2). One set comprises the vertical circles and the other the horizontal circles or hoops. The vertical forces are entirely compressive. The hoop forces are in compression so long as the angle subtended at the centre of the vertical circles is less than 104°. In a hemisphere this angle is 180°, and the lower portion of the dome is therefore subject to horizontal hoop tension. The Ancient Romans were unable to perform this analysis, but they must have obtained this result empirically, because the thickness of the dome of the Pantheon (Fig. 1.1) is increased appreciably in its lower portion to a maximum of 7 m (23 ft).

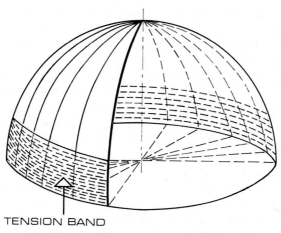

TENSION BAND

Fig. 1.2. The forces in a hemispherical dome may be divided into two sets acting at right angles to one another. One set comprises the vertical circles, or meridians of longitude, and the other comprises the horizontal circles, or hoops, corresponding to the circles of latitude on the earth's surface. The forces along the vertical circles are due to arch action, and are entirely compressive. The hoop forces along the horizontal circles are in compression above an angle of 104°, subtended at the centre of the vertical circles. Below this angle of 104° the hoop forces form a tension band which restrains the dome, which is thus self-balancing. No buttresses are thus required for a hemispherical dome.

The Pantheon, like most important Roman buildings of that period, was built of concrete (Section 2.6). This differed from modern concrete; the coarse aggregate consisted of large pieces, which were laid in horizontal layers; the cement mortar was then poured in the spaces between the stones. Because of the arrangement of the concrete aggregate in horizontal layers, it has sometimes been assumed that the dome is a corbelled structure. However, the cement ties the stones into a composite material, so that the structure is a true dome.

The structural sizes of the Pantheon, and of most other surviving important buildings of Ancient Rome, are conservative. Slave labour was readily available, and the penalties for failure were severe.

1.3. BYZANTINE AND MUSLIM DOMES, ARCHES AND VAULTS

The Roman Empire divided into an Eastern and a Western Empire in AD 395. The Western Empire came to an end in 476, but the Eastern, or Byzantine, Empire continued until 1453. A great dome was built in its capital, Constantinople, in a mere six years, from AD 531 to 537, over the church of St Sophia (Hagia Sophia, Aya Sofia). Its construction has been described by the historian Procopius [12]. The interior surface of the dome is part of a sphere, but less than a hemisphere. It subtends an angle of approximately 143° at the centre of curvature, so that (Fig. 1.2) only a little hoop tension develops. However, the dome produces horizontal reactions or thrusts, which must be absorbed.

The reactions of a hemispherical dome are purely vertical (Fig. 1.3(a)). In the shallow dome of St Sophia there is very little hoop tension, and the horizontal components of the reactions are absorbed on two sides by massive masonry buttresses, and on the other two by semidomes. Byzantine domes are generally shallow (Fig. 1.3(b)), as are many Muslim domes, and the resulting horizontal thrusts are always absorbed by buttresses and semidomes, which surround the central domes.

The dome of St Sophia is smaller in diameter (33 m or 108 ft) than that of the Pantheon, but its height is greater, because it is supported on four great pillars. In these lead was used as a binding material for the masonry instead of mortar [12].

The circle is not as efficient a structural shape for the masonry dome or arch as the catenary, the shape assumed by a cable hanging under its own weight. It conforms to the equation, $y = c \cosh (x/c)$, where x and y are the horizontal and vertical coordinates, and c is a constant. The shape of the catenary differs only slightly from the shape of a parabola of the same sag and span.

Since the cable is in pure tension, the catenary arch is in pure compression under its own weight. This result was derived by David

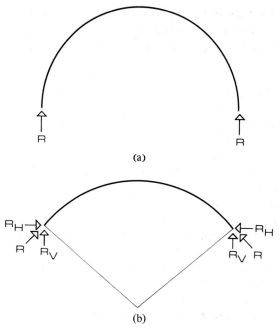

Fig. 1.3.   The reactions, *R*, of a hemispherical dome (a) are purely vertical. The horizontal thrust normally exerted by a hemispherical arch at its support is absorbed in a hemispherical dome by the tension band (Fig. 1.2). In a shallow dome (b) the reactions, *R*, are inclined to the vertical. They can be resolved into a vertical component, R_V, transmitted to the piers or other supports, and a horizontal reaction, R_H, which must be absorbed by buttresses or semidomes.

Gregory, Professor of Astronomy at Oxford University, and published in the Philosophical Transactions of the Royal Society in 1697. However, empirically the result had been known in general terms a thousand years earlier, and it has been rediscovered whenever the only materials available are too weak for building circular arches which are inevitably subject to some bending.

In Mesopotamia good building stone is scarce, and so is fuel for burning bricks. As a result mud-bricks and lightly burnt bricks have been extensively used, and the catenary arch was presumably discovered as a result of using these inferior materials. The largest structure of this type was built about AD 550 in the reign of King Khosrau I of Persia at Ctesiphon, which was then the capital; it is now a suburb of Baghdad. The Great Hall of the Palace is a catenary-shaped vault 34 m (112 ft) high and spanning 26 m (85 ft), and it is still standing. It is built of brick, 7 m (23 ft) thick at the base, laid in horizontal courses. The weight of the material is sufficient to cause it to act like a catenary, rather than a corbelled, vault.

The catenary-shaped circular mud huts found in various parts of Central Africa to the present day are based on the same structural principle.

Catenary-shaped arches are found in Seljuk architecture in Turkey and Iran, alongside pointed arches. The pointed arch is probably a compromise between the structurally efficient catenary arch, which is difficult to build because of its complex geometry, and the structurally less efficient circular arch. By using two intersecting circular arcs a shape resembling a catenary can be obtained.

Christopher Wren, whose job as Surveyor of Works required him to maintain the fabric of many Gothic cathedrals, thought that the pointed Gothic arch derived from Saracen architecture. The Crusaders must have seen pointed arches in Jerusalem and elsewhere in the Holy Land, and they may even have brought back Saracens proficient in their construction.

1.4. GOTHIC STRUCTURE

While architecture flourished in the Middle East, both in the Byzantine Empire and in the new Muslim states, it declined in western Europe following the fall of the Western Roman Empire. In the 9th century there was a revival, and in the 12th century there occurred in France, and shortly afterwards in Britain, the subtle change now known as Gothic. Gothic cathedrals have always fascinated engineers because of the extraordinary slenderness of some parts of the structure.

When the builder was liable to be put to death, in accordance with Hammurabi's code, he had every encouragement to oversize his structural members. Even though later building codes were less drastic, there was no great inducement to structural economy in the Ancient World. Labour was plentiful, and the buildings which survive were mostly financed by powerful rulers.

The Gothic cathedrals were paid for by relatively small cities or bishoprics, or by kings with very limited resources. The *pax Romana* had given way to constant warfare, which consumed wealth previously available for building. The Christian religion had virtually abolished slavery. Thus the economic use of stone in Gothic cathedrals, and their assembly from pieces of stone much smaller than those commonly used in Roman and Egyptian masonry, was at least partly due to shortage of labour and of money.

The strength of religious feeling was another important factor. Collapses of vaults and towers were not uncommon, and they were

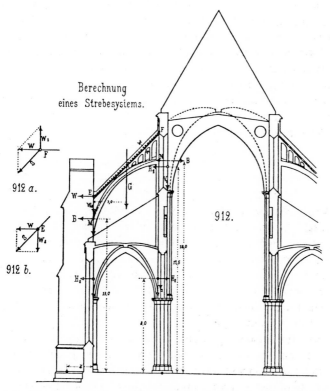

Fig. 1.4. The forces in the buttresses and columns of a Gothic cathedral according to a 19th century treatise *Lehrbuch der Gothischen Konstruktion* by G. G. Ungewitter.

given supernatural explanations [38], and so was the survival of structural members which, by present-day standards, are clearly undersized. The builder was not necessarily held responsible for either failure or success. His own religious conviction may have encouraged him to place a faith in divine providence which modern building codes expressly forbid.

Experience was also important. The Gothic style changed slowly over a period of three centuries, and the structural members gradually became more slender. The Gothic master masons travelled widely. Etienne de Bonneul, the designer of the cathedral of Uppsala, in Sweden, came from Paris, Villard [34] went to Hungary, and William of Sens, in France, became master mason of Canterbury Cathedral. The experience gathered by these masters may have been passed on within the organisation of the masonic lodges, but we do not know what rules were devised for the structural sizes of the Gothic cathedrals. However, it is certain that they were geometric constructions or proportional rules, and not based on statics which was unknown at the time.

The Gothic tradition declined during the Renaissance, and when the Gothic style was revived in the 19th century, structural analyses were made with the aid of the new science of statics. Certain features of Gothic architecture could by that time be analysed, particularly the buttresses and the flying buttresses (Fig. 1.4). The elastic theory (Section 2.4) stipulates that if the masonry joints were not to open up (Fig. 1.5), the resultant of the thrust exerted by the flying buttress (Fig. 1.6) must lie within the middle third. Gothic masons were, of course, concerned with collapse and not with elastic stresses, and this condition is more correctly represented by the 20th century theory of ultimate strength design (Section 3.9). From this it can be shown that the buttress does not collapse so long as the resultant is within the section, instead of within the middle third of the section; thus the middle-third rule gives a substantial safety margin.

Viollet-le-Duc [35] in the 1840s and 1850s restored French cathedrals utilising the new structural theory, including Amiens, Notre Dame of Paris and St Denis, the first Gothic cathedral. Other architects at the same time restored Gothic cathedrals in Britain [36] and elsewhere. In the process many structural features were greatly strengthened, perhaps excessively so. Since there are no detailed

Fig. 1.5. The middle-third rule: when a load is placed outside the middle third of an elastic block, tension develops on the opposite side. In a masonry structure the joints open up.

records of many of the restorations, it is impossible to say now in some instances what were the structural sizes of the original cathedrals. Collapses of medieval cathedrals were not uncommon prior to the 19th-century restorations; the spire of Chichester Cathedral telescoped into the body of the church as recently as 1861. While the increased structural sizes of the restorers may in some cases have been excessive, they put an end to major failures.

It has been argued, notably by Pol Abraham [39], that in the process of restoration many cathedrals acquired flying buttresses and pinnacles where there were none before, and which were in fact unnecessary.

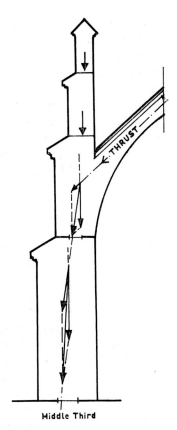

Fig. 1.6.   The theory of the buttress, developed in the 19th century, based on keeping the resultant force within the middle third.

The factor of safety of the original Gothic structures was very variable. Since the master masons had no means of structural sizing (except possibly empirical rules) and they tended towards a light design (perhaps for economic, perhaps for artistic or religious reasons), there were bound to be some structural members which were grossly undersized and collapsed immediately; there were some which had a very small factor of safety and might fall down later if circumstances were unfavourable (for example, a high wind, decay of stone of poor durability, a minor repair which altered the load distribution, or settlement of the foundations, which caused a collapse at a later time); there were some which had a factor of safety which we now consider appropriate; and there were some which were grossly oversized. In an overdesigned structure, or even in one with an adequate factor of safety, the vault would not necessarily fail if the flying buttress was removed or missing, and conversely, the flying buttress would not necessarily fall down if the vault was removed. Thus many Gothic cathedrals damaged by war did not collapse completely when an essential part of the structure was destroyed. There are Gothic ruins which according to Viollet-le-Duc lack supporting members, but have remained standing for centuries.

Nevertheless, most Gothic cathedrals require flying buttresses. If the vault was high, the pillars of the nave would have been enormous without flying buttresses across the aisles, particularly if there was a steep timber roof or a tower to transmit wind loads. It did not really require any knowledge of statics to recognise that need. The flying buttress is merely a permanent and larger form of an inclined timber prop used during the construction of a tall masonry wall.

The structural function of the pinnacle is more debatable. The upward surge of Gothic sculpture could by itself account for the pinnacle as an artistic, rather than a structural feature. On the other hand, there is a tendency for the flying buttress to shear the top of the vertical buttress (Fig. 1.6), and this shear causes tensile stresses in the masonry at about 45° to the line of thrust. Stone is weak in tension, and it is then necessary either to make the buttress thicker, or to cancel out the tension by compression, produced by the weight of the pinnacle above the flying buttress. Some pinnacles are certainly needed for structural safety.

Having discovered the need for flying buttresses and pinnacles, the Gothic designers used them as part of the sculpture. They became stylised, and in some later churches they were superfluous.

1.5. THE DOMES OF THE RENAISSANCE

The Italian Renaissance, which started in Florence in the early 15th century, was due to a revival of interest in classical science, art and architecture, and the consequent rejection of the 'barbarism' of Gothic. However, Renaissance architecture was not a copy of Roman architecture.

The first dome of the Renaissance was also its biggest and most daring. The cathedral of S. Maria del Fiore, generally known as the Duomo or House (of the Lord), was started in 1296 by Arnolfo di Cambio. The octagonal dome was probably his concept. The foundations of the great octagon were erected in 1366, and in the following year a large brick model of the entire cathedral was built; views of this model appear in contemporary frescoes. The general shape of the dome was therefore established before Brunelleschi's time, but whether anybody had a scheme for erecting a dome with a span of 42 m (138 ft), and much higher than any ever built, is not known.

Brunelleschi divided the dome into an inner and an outer shell, with a space in between, which can be used for access and maintenance, but which also provides a large lever arm for any bending moments within the dome. He justified this on the ground that it would prevent the ingress of water which might spoil the frescoes on the inside of the dome; whether he considered the extra stiffness which it would give to the dome is not known. He provided a number of main and intermediate ribs to absorb the vertical forces along the meridians, which are entirely compressive. In addition he provided a number of chains to absorb hoop tension. There are six stone chains, shown in Fig. 1.7 by the numbers 14 to 20. They consist of blocks of sandstone joined together by lead-covered iron clamps which transmit the tension from one block to the next, completing the chain. Number 21 is a chain of chestnut logs interconnected with rectangular plates of oak, and fastened with tin-plated bolts. The dome therefore has quite a generous amount of tension reinforcement.

Two centuries later Christopher Wren adopted an entirely different solution for St Paul's Cathedral. The dome itself is tall, and it is surmounted by a tall masonry lantern weighing 700 tonnes. It would have been impossible to build a dome with this ratio of rise to span and with such a heavy concentrated load on top without either buttresses or a great deal of reinforcement. Wren did not want the first, because it was Gothic, and he may not have known of Brunelleschi's stone chains. The loadbearing structure is a brick cone

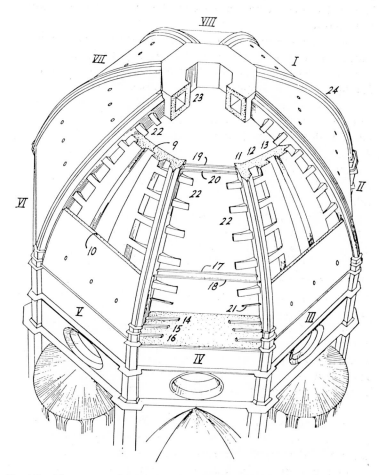

Fig. 1.7. The masonry fabric of the cupola of the Duomo of Florence, drawn by G. Rich in 1969. (From Ref. 41, p. 35, reproduced by permission of MIT Press.) I–VIII, the eight sides of the dome are partly removed to show the interior framework; 9 and 10, inner and outer masonry shells; 11–13, main and intermediate ribs; 14–20, stone chains; 21, timber chain; 22, horizontal arches; 23, opening at the top of the dome; 24, exterior ridges over main ribs.

between an inner and outer dome (Fig. 1.8). The outer dome was a timber truss resting on the brick cone (now rebuilt in reinforced concrete). The inner dome is of brick, and carries merely its own weight. The loadbearing cone is in fact very close to the catenary for this particular load system, and, although Wren does not say anywhere how he arrived at it, there is circumstantial evidence to suggest that he solved the problem in terms of the catenary.

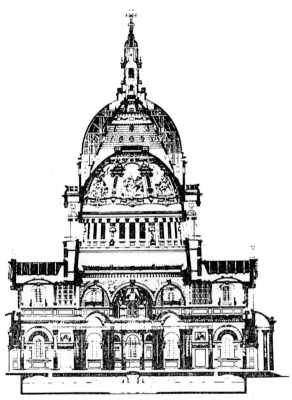

Fig. 1.8.   Cross section of St Paul's Cathedral, London, looking east. Although the outer dome, which is lead-covered, looks remarkably like that of St Peter's Basilica in Rome, on which it is presumably modelled, it is not, like St Peter's, a loadbearing structure. It is a timber frame supported by the brick cone between the two domes, which closely approximates to the shape of the catenary for the load system constituted by its own weight, that of the timber frame, and the heavy masonry lantern. (From a drawing by Arthur F. E. Poley in Ref. 44.)

If we hang a chain of beads from two nails, it assumes the catenary shape for its loading system, and it is then in pure tension. If we freeze this shape and turn it upside down (Fig. 1.9), we obtain a catenary arch which is in pure compression (Section 1.3). The problem was raised in 1670 at a meeting of the Royal Society by Robert Hooke, of Hooke's Law fame (Section 1.6), who was a close collaborator of Wren. In 1697, the year in which the construction of the dome of St Paul's began, David Gregory, who had succeeded Wren as Professor of Astronomy at Oxford (Section 1.3), published a paper which established that a catenary was the correct figure for an arch which was to be in pure compression.

It is therefore likely that the cone was designed as a catenary. It was an effective solution, since the structure of St Paul's is the thinnest and lightest of all the masonry domes built before the days of reinforced concrete (Section 4.9), and it has never given any trouble.

The older dome of St Peter's Basilica in Rome was less satisfactory. The original design was by Donato Bramante, and the foundation stone was laid in 1506. Bramante's design was conservative: a solid hemispherical dome, thickened in the lower portion, with steps showing outside, as in the Pantheon (Fig. 1.1), which was clearly the inspiration. The dome actually built was designed by Michelangelo, who became the fifth architect of St Peter's when he was already 72 years of age. He sent to Florence for details of Brunelleschi's dome, and changed the design to a much thinner double shell (Fig. 1.10). On his death he left drawings and a model, both of which survive [42]. Giacomo della Porta finished the dome in 1590, substantially in accordance with this design.

The predominant material of the dome is brick. There are three iron chains around the base to absorb the hoop tension [96]. It has repeatedly been suggested that there are in addition some iron clamps joining the blocks of masonry, as in Florence, but they have not been found, and they are not on the drawings.

The tension reinforcement was insufficient, because the dome showed alarming cracks by 1740 and the Pope called in a number of experts. The most interesting report was the one received from Giovanni Poleni, Professor of Natural Philosophy (*i.e.* Physics), at the University of Padua. Poleni argued that the vertical cracks in the

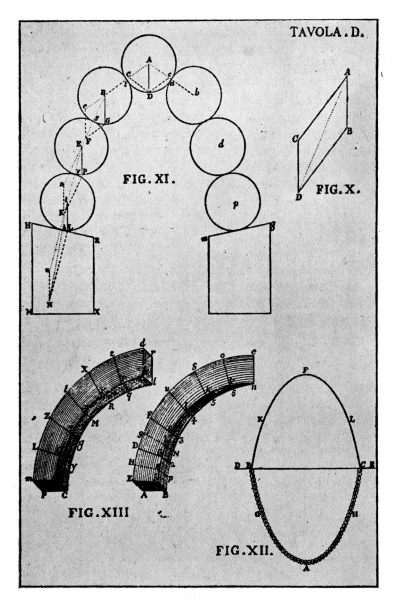

Fig. 1.9. Illustration from *Memorie istoriche della Gran Cupola del Templo Vaticano*, by Giovanni Poleni, Padua 1748. The parallelogram of forces (X); the masonry arch idealised as a catenary of smooth spheres (XI); the use of the catenary for the solution of the masonry arch (XII and XIII).

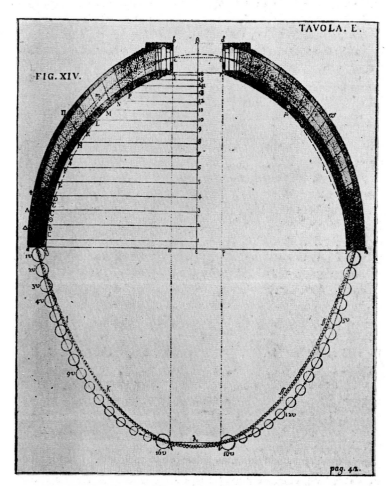

Fig. 1.10. Illustration from *Memorie istoriche*, by Poleni: The catenary chain for a dome of uniform weight, and for the dome of St Peter's Basilica in Rome; the line of thrust represented by the catenary superimposed on the cross section of the dome.

dome would divide it into a number of orange-slice segments, and provided that each of these segments was safe as an arch, then the entire dome was also safe. Poleni used Gregory's theory of the catenary, published 40 years earlier (Fig. 1.9). He made up a string of beads, the weight of each bead being proportional to the weight of a unit portion of a standard orange-slice segment. He determined the shape of the catenary experimentally by hanging the beads from two pins representing the span. Poleni then superimposed that catenary on the cross section of the dome, found that it lay entirely inside (Fig. 1.10), and therefore concluded that the dome was safe, provided that the hoop force at the base was sufficient to prevent the orange slices from spreading [71]. It was clearly not sufficient, and in 1744 five additional tie chains were added to the dome; it has given no serious trouble since.

Thomas Young, of Young's modulus fame (Section 1.6), was the first to state, without proof, that tension would develop in a spherical dome only if its span exceeded $\frac{11}{14}$ of the diameter, that is, if the angle subtended at the centre of the sphere is more than 104° (Fig. 1.2). He published this result in 1807 in a *Course of Lectures on Natural Philosophy and the Mechanical Arts*, which contained the substance of his lectures delivered at the Royal Institution of London. The proof was given by Edmund Beckett Denison (later Sir Edmund Beckett and later still the Rt. Hon. Lord Grimphorpe) in a paper on the theory of domes in the Memoirs of the Royal Institute of British Architects in 1871. He proved Young's statement, without mentioning Young, and showed that the stability of the masonry dome depended only on the ratio of thickness to span, which is correct. For a hemispherical dome he stated that the ratio of span to thickness should not exceed 20, and this also accords with modern research [74]. This means that a 42 m (138 ft) diameter hemispherical dome requires a thickness of 2·1 m (7 ft), including the space between the two shells of a double-shelled dome. The theory is based on simple statics. Denison stated that he invented the theory, and that it was the first time that it had been correctly stated. As far as the author has been able to ascertain, the claim is correct.

Denison pointed out that hoop forces could be resisted only by a great mass of material, as in the Pantheon, or else by buttresses or by metal ties. He therefore predicted the demise of masonry domes in favour of those of iron (Ref. 1, article *Dome*). In fact a number of iron domes were built during the later 19th century (Section 4.5).

Denison's solution came too late for masonry domes, which had already lost popularity in the 1870s. In fact none of the masonry domes which followed St Paul's of London ever reached the same span.

1.6. THE BEGINNINGS OF THE STUDY OF STRUCTURAL MECHANICS

The beginnings of structural mechanics can be traced back to Ancient Greece. Archimedes discovered the principle of the lever, and was able to determine the centre of gravity of simple geometric figures. Most of the significant practical applications were, however, in the field of military engineering which was then, as it is today, given particular attention. The simple machines employed by the Greeks and the Romans in the transport and erection of heavy blocks of stone were mainly by-products of military equipment [86].

The failure of the Greek philosophers to put their considerable scientific knowledge to more practical use was to a large extent due to a reluctance to consider the strength of a building as being worthy of scientific study. Their most elaborate mechanisms, apparently deliberately, served no significant engineering purpose. Hero of Alexandria, who lived some time between the 1st century BC and the 1st century AD, described several of them in his *Pneumatika*. One was a machine for dispensing holy water (Fig. 1.11). Another was a rotating mechanism operated by steam jets, which was based on the same principle as the 19th century reaction turbine, but was not intended to generate any power. Perhaps the most ingenious device in Hero's *Pneumatika* was an automatic machine for opening the doors of a temple as if the god had done so himself. The priest lit the fire on the altar and then withdrew. The fire generated steam in a boiler below. This forced water through a syphon, which consequently filled a vessel suspended from a rope. The pull on the rope rotated a column which through a gear opened the doors of the temple.

Medieval scholars had got no further than a solution of the law

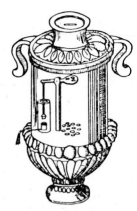

Fig. 1.11.   Coin-in-the-slot machine for dispensing holy water, described by Hero of Alexandria. It contained a lever mechanism not unlike that of a modern vending machine. This operated a piston to release a measured quantity of holy water.

of the inclined plane, credited to Jordanus Nemorarius, a 13th century monk. He considered the inclined plane in terms of 'diluted gravity', the flatter the plane, the greater the dilution of gravity [56].

Before any progress could be made towards an analysis of the forces acting on a structure, it was necessary to define the notion of force as a vectorial unit, *i.e.* as a quantity having both magnitude and direction. This was a task which called for a considerable effort of abstraction. Leonardo da Vinci was the first to solve this problem. Born in Florence in 1452, he was one of the most versatile men of the Renaissance. He published nothing during his lifetime, but he left his extensive notes to his friend and pupil Francesco Melzi, after whose death the notebooks were dispersed; some have been lost. Leonardo, who was left-handed, wrote in a writing which ordinary persons can only read in a mirror and he used many abbreviations. Most of his writing has been transcribed only during the 20th century.

Leonardo considered the condition of equilibrium of two inclined strings carrying a weight (Fig. 1.12). He noted that the pull in a string could be ascertained by hanging it over a pulley, and balancing it with a weight. If one hung a weight from two inclined strings, and set out the pull in the strings and the weight carried by them to scale,

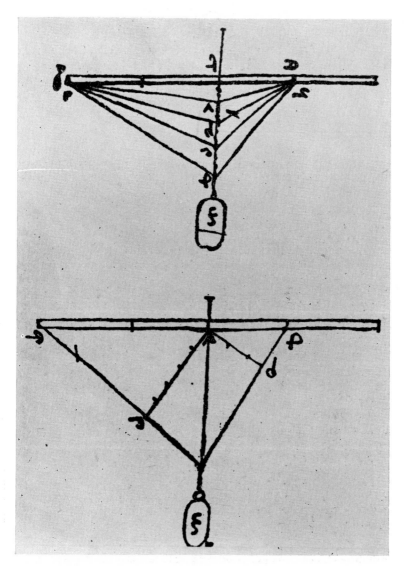

Fig. 1.12. The parallelogram of forces (From Leonardo da Vinci's Notebooks, Arundel MS, No. 283, folio 1, verso, in the British Museum. The explanation quoted in the text appears in MS E in the *Institut de France*, folio 60, verso).

one obtained a parallelogram [96]. This is the parallelogram of forces which, together with Archimedes' lever principle, forms the basis of statics. It was rediscovered by Simon Stevin of Bruges (Belgium) in 1586. There is no reason to believe that he knew what was in Leonardo's notebooks.

The discovery of elasticity is credited to Robert Hooke, the friend of Christopher Wren. In 1678 he described his experiments in a lecture delivered to the Royal Society, and he published them in the same year under the title *De Potentia Restitutiva*. He explained that 'all springy bodies whatsoever, whether metal, wood, stones, baked earth, hair, horns, silk, bones, sinews, glass and the like' can be extended by a force. When the force is removed they recover their original length. Moreover the extension is directly proportional to

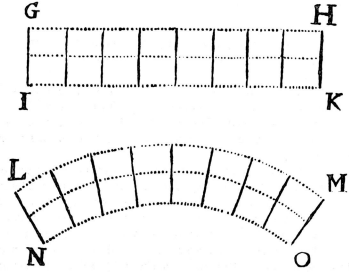

Fig. 1.13.   An illustration from Hooke's *De Potentia Restitutiva, or of Spring Explaining the Powers of Springing Bodies* (published by John Martyn, London, 1678), showing a piece of dry wood bent in such a way that the top of the beam is extended and the bottom compressed. The originally plane and parallel sections remain plane and converge on a common centre of curvature. This assumption was subsequently used by Navier as the geometric basis for his theory of bending (Section 2.3). He may or may not have derived it from Hooke. Hooke used the figure to illustrate springiness, not to solve the theory of bending.

the force applied. Hooke's Law is now expressed in the form 'force is proportional to extension', or 'stress is proportional to strain' [68].

Hooke's Law makes two distinct statements, one about the recovery of the elastic deformation of structural material, and the other about the linear relation between the applied load and the elastic deformation.

The constant in Hooke's Law was first defined by Thomas Young in 1807 in his *Course of Lectures* already mentioned in Section 1.5; it is now frequently called Young's modulus.

One of Hooke's examples of a springy body in *De Potentia Restitutiva* was a piece of dry wood bent in such a way that the top of the beam was extended and the bottom compressed (Fig. 1.13). The originally plane and parallel vertical sections remain plane and converge on a common centre of curvature. This later became the basis of the theory of elastic bending (Section 2.3).

1.7. THE AGE OF REASON AND THE FOUNDATIONS OF THE CLASSICAL THEORY OF STRUCTURES

Experimental determination of the physical properties of materials can be traced with certainty to the early Renaissance, and some tests were probably carried out earlier. Leonardo da Vinci described in his Notebooks a machine for testing the tensile strength of a wire [96].

The relative lack of progress in determining the physical properties of materials during the next two centuries was due mainly to attempts to test full-size pieces of material with dead weights, which proved very expensive (Fig. 1.14). With the development of the lever testing machine in the 18th century systematic testing became practicable, and in 1729 Petrus van Musschenbroek, Professor of Physics at the University of Leyden (Holland), published in *Physicae experimentales et geometricae dissertationes* the first comprehensive table of the strength of various materials. Musschenbroek's data were held in high regard throughout the 18th and the early 19th century, and they were still reprinted in the Sixth Edition of Peter Barlow's *A Treatise on the Strength of Materials*, published in 1867.

All the elements were now available for a theory of the strength

Fig. 1.14.   Bending test, using cannon balls for weights. (From *An Essay on the Strength of Timber*, by Peter Barlow, Professor at the Royal Military Academy, published by A. J. Taylor, London, 1817.)

of structures. The parallelogram of forces and the lever principle provided the basis for determining the internal forces within a structure caused by the loads it carried, Hooke's Law made it possible to determine the elastic deformation caused by these internal forces, and Musschenbroek's tables gave the necessary information on the strength of the structural material.

A number of theories for the strength of beams and columns were produced during the 18th century, but they did not produce a useful theory of structural design. This was largely due to the complexity of the architectural structures of the time. It would have been easier to analyse Ancient Egyptian or Greek structures. Even with simpler structures, however, like the timber trusses of Palladio (Section 3.1), scientific design depended on the definition of a limiting stress.

Since measurements of elastic deformation were possible only in very simple cases before the 19th century, the early elastic theories were generally checked by tests to destruction. Elastic behaviour and failure, however, are concerned with essentially different properties of the same material, and the resulting discrepancies in the experiments caused much confusion in the 17th and 18th centuries.

It was only during the 19th century that the perfection of extensometers for measuring small strains put the elastic theory on a sound experimental basis, and the verification by tests to destruction ceased to be necessary. Hooke's Law became the basis of an elaborate and highly mathematical theory of elasticity which could be used with confidence without constant resort to experiment.

In recent years, however, we have developed qualms about the soundness of elasticity as the main basis of structural design, and have recognised in the confusion of the pioneers of the Age of Reason a basic structural problem which requires further consideration.

Chapter 2

One-Dimensional Structures, and the Invention of Steel and of Reinforced Concrete Construction

> Settlers at a distance from the towns, who find it difficult to procure skilled workmen, I strongly recommend to try this economic building; and even for stations in the bush when, as is often the case, limestone is to be found. Concrete buildings would be nearly, if not quite, as cheap as log huts; and whilst being infinitely more comfortable, they would be fireproof, set at defiance all the attempts of the blacks to burn them, and thus, in case of an attack, enable their inmates to hold out until help arrives.
>
> *Herschel Babbage writing to* The Builder *from Australia in* 1860

2.1. THE BEGINNINGS OF ENGINEERED STRUCTURES

The emergence of modern structural engineering depended on the development of a simple and accurate theory of design, and on the mass production of materials with the requisite properties; both were needed before any real progress could be made.

While structural mechanics had been studied continuously since the 16th century, the most significant developments occurred in France after the foundation of the École des Ponts et Chaussées in 1747. Following the Revolution the schools and universities of the *Ancien Régime* were discontinued, and the École Polytechnique, founded in 1795, became the main centre of theoretical mechanics.

Somewhat surprisingly, one of the most difficult problems, the buckling of columns, was solved by Euler as early as 1757. Study of the theory of bending, commenced by Galileo in the early 17th century, extended over two centuries. The analysis of the truss, generally regarded as one of the simplest problems in modern structural mechanics, received no serious consideration until the middle of the 19th century.

In the 18th century cast iron and wrought iron were being produced in England on a commercial scale. For the first time durable materials with good tensile strength became available in large quantities for use in building. The new materials, moreover, could be shaped with considerable ease during manufacture, and possessed the ideal elastic properties assumed in the theory.

The first major iron structure, a cast iron arch bridge, was built over the Severn at Coalbrookdale in England, in 1779 by Abraham Darby [109]. This bridge has a span of 30 m (98 ft), and is still standing. Its construction was preceded by lengthy deliberations during which designs in stone and a combination of iron and stone were at first favoured. The design eventually adopted is reminiscent of a stone arch, in which the mortar joints are replaced by the iron ribs, and the blocks of masonry become voids. The connections of the iron elements are based on standard timber joints. A more logical use of iron only developed at the end of the 18th century, when the material was increasingly used in the construction of bridges and buildings.

The possession of the right material proved at first more important than theoretical knowledge, and most of the early development of building in iron and steel took place in Britain. During much of this time Britain and France were at war, which discouraged intellectual contact and caused ideas originating on the other side of the English Channel to be treated with some disdain. In consequence, British engineers of the late 18th and early 19th centuries were fifty years behind the French school in their theoretical work, and relied largely on load tests for the verification of their designs. English structural engineering books during the early 19th century placed strong emphasis on practical experience, and sometimes referred to the use of mathematics in slighting terms. The discrepancy between French theory and English practical experience is noted on a number of occasions; usually it is the result of attempts to use an elastic theory for verifying results obtained from tests to destruction.

2.2. EARLY STRUCTURES IN IRON AND STEEL

The advent of iron resulted in a return to the earliest and simplest form of structure, the beam supported by columns. Whereas the stone lintels of Greek and Renaissance architecture rarely spanned more than a few feet, iron beams were capable of spanning the aisle of a medieval cathedral. Being simply supported, they could do so, moreover, without exerting a lateral thrust.

The use of the new material was confined mainly to the industrial buildings, which began to make their appearance in the late 18th century. The population of Britain increased rapidly during the late 18th and the early 19th century, and so did the number of factories and of buildings generally. The designers of industrial buildings usually did not engage in work of a more conventionally architectural character, and two separate professions began to emerge, which organised themselves formally: the Institution of Civil Engineers was founded in 1818, and the Royal Institute of British Architects in 1834.

The economic basis for the large-scale use of iron in buildings was, in the first instance, the need for fireproof construction. The buildings most at risk were the new textile mills. A typical mill was five or six storeys high in order to bring all the machinery as close as possible to the source of power, which was at first a water-wheel and later a single large steam engine. The power was transmitted from this prime mover to shafts, and from the shafts to the machines by belting. The longer the belting, the greater the loss of power. This method of power transmission had a low efficiency and it generated an appreciable amount of heat which was a fire hazard. The cotton presented another hazard, and there were many fires in timber-framed mills. It was, however, not uncommon to span across the entire width of the mill, up to 9 m (30 ft) with timber beams 300 mm (12 in) square. Some of these mills still survive in Derbyshire where Arkwright and Strutt built their first cotton mill.

'Fireproof' structures were first built by William Strutt, the son of Arkwright's partner, in 1792. He substituted brick jack arches for the timber floor, and protected the timber beams with plaster or tiles (Fig. 2.1). This greatly increased the weight, and he inserted cast iron columns, generally at 2·7 m (9 ft) centres to reduce the span.

A few years later Strutt, Bage and Boulton built mills with complete iron frames. The cast iron girders had flanges at the base to serve as a support for the brick jack arches (Fig. 2.1). We do not know whether the structural advantage of using material as far as possible from the neutral axis was understood; however, cast iron

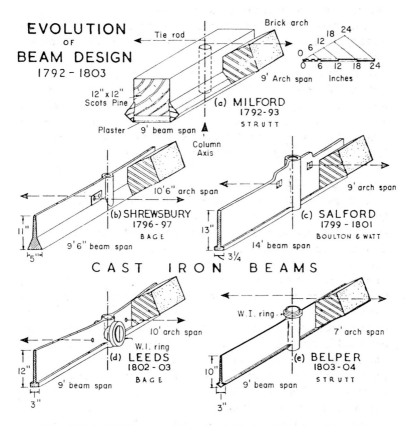

Fig. 2.1. Fire-resistant factory floor structures used in the late 18th and early 19th century. The frame (a) had cast iron columns, which carried timber beams, protected by plaster underneath and brick tiles above. These supported brick jack arches tied with wrought iron bars to absorb the horizontal thrust. The spandrels were filled with rubble, sand or weak concrete. Later cast iron beams supported on cast iron columns were used to improve the fire-resistance ((b) to (e)). The cast iron beams had flanges at their base to serve as support for the brick jack arches. (From Ref. 107.)

beams deliberately moulded in I-shape started to appear in the following decade, and Tredgold in 1824 explained the economic advantages to be derived from their use [109].

The architectural use of cast iron was mainly limited to ornamental work. The elaborate, and sometimes beautiful, balcony screens of old houses in New Orleans, Melbourne and Sydney (Fig. 5.1) are typical examples. There were only a few architects in the first half of the century who used cast iron as a structural material. John Nash employed it in the 1821 additions to Buckingham Palace, and more extensively in the Royal Pavilion in Brighton, where the unusually tall and slender columns in the kitchen are shaped as palm trees. Victor Louis used iron in the Théâtre Français, Sydney Smirke in the Reading Room of the British Museum and Henri Labrouste in the Reading Room of the Bibliothèque Nationale in Paris (Section 4.5). Cast iron columns in public buildings were generally ornate, and frequently imitated classical forms.

The columns were notably more successful than the cast iron beams, partly because the material due to its high compressive strength is more suitable for columns, and partly because the ease with which it could be decorated commended it to the Victorian age. Columns modelled on one of the classical orders were soon used in industrial buildings, and the manufacture of cast iron columns in Britain ceased only during World War I, when the facilities were required for armament production; cast iron beams became obsolete well before the end of the 19th century.

In 1847 Henry Fielder obtained a patent for making compound beams by riveting together cast and wrought iron sections, plates and angles. Wrought iron cost twice as much as cast iron, but it was twice as strong in tension, more consistent in its properties and less susceptible to damage by shock. In 1856 Henry Bessemer invented the process named after him for blowing air through the fluid pig iron, instead of reducing the carbon content by the traditional laborious puddling process.

Steel had until that time been a very expensive material, because it could only be made by reducing the carbon content of cast iron, or by increasing the carbon content of wrought iron. Bessemer's invention drastically reduced the price of steel and made it competitive with cast iron and wrought iron. Since steel combined ductility with high strength, it soon replaced both cast iron and wrought iron for most structural applications.

In 1885 rolled steel joists were produced for the first time, in Britain by Dorman Long and Co., and in America by Carnegie, Phipps and Co. They were first employed in the same year in the upper floors of the Home Insurance Building in Chicago, the lower floors having been built with wrought iron beams (Section 2.4).

The 1880s were an important decade for steel. In 1883 Sir Benjamin Baker commenced the construction of the Firth of Forth Bridge (Fig. 3.4) near Edinburgh (completed in 1890) whose clear span of 520 m (1706 ft) established steel as the ideal material for long-span structures. In 1885 William le Baron Jenney built the first skeleton-framed building in Chicago which, as already mentioned, used steel in its upper floors as superior to wrought iron. In 1889 the Galerie des Machines, designed by the architect Ferdinand Dutert and the engineer Cottançin, was built for the Paris International Exhibition of that year. It set a new record for a span in a building (113 m or 371 ft). By the turn of the century steel had become accepted as the best material for large-scale construction.

2.3. THE THEORY OF BENDING

While virtually all the initial practical development leading up to the modern steel frame took place in the English-speaking countries in little more than a century, the theory of bending was being perfected in France.

Since the bending problem is of such fundamental importance, it is not surprising to find reference to it in Leonardo da Vinci's Notebooks. Galileo, however, gave the first solution.

He observed that a stone cantilever (Fig. 2.2) failed at the support AB. The point B thus formed the fulcrum of two levers: the load E acted on one of these levers, BC, and the resistance of the beam acted on the other lever, AB. Galileo assumed that the resistance of the beam was a tensile force, and he thus assumed a uniform tensile stress (Fig. 2.3(a)). Using modern notation, this gives the equation

$$M = WL = \tfrac{1}{2}fbd^2 \tag{2.1}$$

where M is the bending moment, W is the load, L is the span, b is

Fig. 2.2.   Test on a cantilevered beam (from Galileo Galilei, *Due Nove Scienze*, Elzevier, Leiden, 1638, *see* Ref. 70). Galileo assumed that the weight *E* produced a tensile force across the section AB, resulting in rupture of the cantilever at the support.

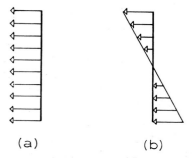

(a)   (b)

Fig. 2.3.   Stress distribution in a beam (a) according to Galileo's theory (Fig. 2.2 and eqn. 2.1), and (b) according to Navier's theory (Fig. 1.13 and eqn. 2.2). Galileo assumed that the cantilever was subject to an internal tensile force, which implies uniform stress distribution. Navier assumed that the material deformed elastically and obeyed Hooke's Law, and that plane sections remained plane; this implies stress distribution varying uniformly from maximum tension at the top to maximum compression at the bottom of the cantilever.

the width of the beam, d is the depth of the beam and f is the force per unit area, or stress, in the material.

Thus Galileo found correctly that the resistance is proportional to the first power of the width and the second power of the depth, and inversely proportional to the distance of the load from the support. However, his answer is three times the true value.

In the 1660s Edmé Mariotte was charged with the design of the water supply pipes for the Palace of Versailles. He carried out tension tests and bending tests to determine the strength of the material, and he found that Galileo's bending formula gave a result for the strength of the material which differed from that obtained from the tension tests [68].

He then pointed out that Galileo had implicitly assumed that his cantilever was an inextensible solid. Mariotte argued that even the hardest materials deform under load, and he assumed, with Hooke, that they were elastic, and that the load was proportional to the deformation. He observed that there must be some compression at the bottom of the cantilever. The beam might thus be considered as a bundle of individual fibres, which deformed in tension near the top of the cantilever, and in compression near the bottom.

This is correct, but Mariotte next tried to prove his elastic theory by comparing it with the results of his tests on pipes, which were taken to failure. He made an arithmetic error, and got a factor of $\frac{1}{3}$ where Galileo had obtained a factor of $\frac{1}{2}$; the correct answer is $\frac{1}{6}$. The results obtained from his tests agreed with the incorrect formula which is presumably the explanation of the mistake.

In Mariotte's time it was not possible to derive an ultimate strength theory for bending, only an elastic theory. On the other hand, it was only possible to test for ultimate strength; an elastic theory could not be checked.

Like all his contemporaries, Mariotte was thinking in terms of ultimate strength (Section 3.9). He had conducted a test, and he was deriving a formula to predict the load at which the test specimen would fail. He assumed that the material would behave elastically, with its load proportional to its deformation, right up to the point of failure.

The long history of the solution of the theory of bending has been recorded in detail by Todhunter [67] and by Heyman [71], and more briefly by Timoshenko [68] and by Straub [103]. A number of people came close to solving the problem. The derivation of the theory still used today and bearing his name was published in Paris in 1826 by Louis Marie Henri Navier, in *Résumé des leçons données à l'École des Ponts et Chaussées, sur l'application de la mécanique à l'établissement des constructions et des machines* (Summary of lectures given at the School for Bridges and Roads on the application of mechanics to the design of structures and machines).

Navier assumed that the material was elastic and obeyed Hooke's Law, and that initially plane sections remain plane and converge on a centre of curvature (Fig. 1.13). The second assumption could not be proved until the later part of the 19th century when sufficiently accurate instruments for measuring strain had been developed (Section 4.1). He assumed, like Mariotte, that the individual fibres of the beam could move freely relative to one another, and he showed that the neutral axis passed through the centroid of the cross section (Fig. 2.3(b)).

For the cantilever used by Galileo this gave the formula

$$M = WL = \tfrac{1}{6}fbd^2 \tag{2.2}$$

This theory is valid only as long as the material behaves elastically. Navier considered that structures should behave elastically under the loads they normally carried, so that they would not suffer permanent deformation. The maximum stress should therefore not exceed a stress now called the maximum permissible stress or working stress, which is substantially lower than the stress at which the material ceases to behave elastically.

This was first fixed about 1840 when the British Board of Trade limited the working stress for wrought iron in railway bridges to the average ultimate strength recorded in various tests on wrought iron, divided by four. J. W. M. Rankine, Professor of Engineering at the University of Glasgow, introduced in the 1850s the term *factor of safety* for this divisor. The factor of safety has been progressively reduced from 4 in the 1840s for wrought iron to approximately 1·5 for steel at the present time.

The elastic theory of structures developed during the remainder of the 19th and the early 20th century to provide a quantitative method for the design of structures which could be used without constant resort to full-scale testing. It completely transformed engineering practice, and later architectural design.

2.4. The Conventional Design of Iron Beams and of Steel Frames

By the middle of the 19th century Navier's theory of bending had become generally accepted for the design of iron beams.

The advantages of concentrating the iron in the region where the highest stresses occurred (Fig. 2.3(b)) was known empirically even before the theory of bending had been derived. Tredgold recommended the use of cast iron I-sections in 1824. Wrought iron I-sections were built up from plates and angles with rivets in the early 19th century, and wrought iron I-beams were rolled before 1850.

For an I-section the bending resistance is not so easily calculated. Equation (2.2) may be written

$$M = fZ \qquad (2.3)$$

where Z is the section modulus; for a rectangular section

$$Z = \tfrac{1}{6}bd^2$$

Trade catalogues surviving from the early and middle 19th century show that manufacturers soon found it useful to supply tables of the section moduli of their products, or to give the safe load over various spans for each section. Tredgold included safe-load tables in his book [109].

The bending moment due to a concentrated load W acting on a cantilever of span L (Fig. 2.2) is WL. However, the most common bending problem in 19th-century buildings was that of the simply supported beam carrying a uniformly distributed load (Fig. 2.4), for which the bending moment is

$$M = \tfrac{1}{8}WL \qquad (2.4)$$

Thus the cast iron beams of Fig. 2.1 rested simply on the supporting cast iron columns. When skeleton frames came into use in the 1880s, eqn. (2.4) was still used for the design of the beams. The beams were now no longer resting on the columns, but connected to them through angle cleats, these connections being sufficiently

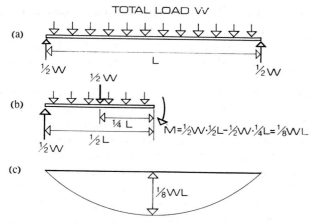

Fig. 2.4.   A simply supported beam of span *L* carrying a uniformly distributed load *W* is shown at (a). To obtain the maximum bending moment we cut the beam at mid-span (b). This half of the beam is now loaded by the end reaction $\frac{1}{2}W$, acting $\frac{1}{2}L$ from mid-span, and the half-load $\frac{1}{2}W$ acting $\frac{1}{4}L$ from mid-span; the bending moment at mid-span is therefore $\frac{1}{8}WL$. The variation of bending moment along the span is shown at (c).

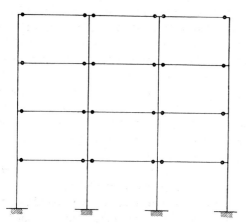

Fig. 2.5.   Assumptions made in the design of a small steel frame under vertical loading. If the steel beams are connected through steel angle cleats to the steel columns, they can be regarded as simply supported on flexible connections, or pin joints. The columns cantilever from the ground.

flexible to justify the assumption that the beams were simply supported on the columns (Fig. 2.5).

The skeleton-framed building developed in Chicago after the Great Fire of 1871, when 18 000 buildings, including the entire city centre, were destroyed.

Although iron was by 1870 commonly used for industrial buildings, designed by engineers, it had found few applications in architect-designed buildings (Section 2.2). Building development in Chicago, however, was not impeded by an architectural tradition. It was far removed from Europe, and more than 1000 km from New York and Boston, where European influence was strong. In the 1830s Chicago had become the birthplace of the balloon frame (Section 6.5), which revolutionised the construction of timber houses and greatly reduced their cost.

The city was rebuilt after the Great Fire with great energy, and the new buildings were made fire-resistant. The population increased from 300 000 in 1870 to a million in 1890.

Fire-protected timber beams were used initially, but the use of iron beams increased rapidly. The exterior brick or stone walls were loadbearing. Cast iron was used for interior columns.

In 1885 William le Baron Jenney built the first skeleton frame in the Home Insurance Building. Cast iron columns were used not merely for the interior columns, but also within the external walls. These columns were designed to carry wrought iron beams, which were in fact used for the lower floors. However, in that year the Carnegie–Phipps Company started to roll the first Bessemer-steel beams (Section 2.2), and these were used in the upper floors.

The passenger lift, or elevator, had come into use in New York in 1857 (Section 5.7), and the first lift had been installed in Chicago in 1870, shortly before the Fire. The major post-fire buildings were all designed as 'elevator buildings', and the use of lifts was an essential precondition for the increase in height. In 1882 the ten-storey Montauk Block was designed by Burnham and Root [55]. By the early 1890s there were more than a dozen buildings exceeding ten storeys in height, and the term 'skyscraper' was coined in 1891 for these tall buildings.

Wind bracing was never used in the tall buildings of the 1870s and 1880s, nor were wind loads considered. The external masonry

walls, which were used even in skeleton-framed buildings, provided
sufficient wind resistance, at least for buildings of less than skyscraper
height.

In 1892 the Capital Building, later known as the Masonic Temple,
set a new record of 21 storeys (92 m or 302 ft). Designed by Burnham
and Root, the building had a steel frame, and crossed wrought iron
bars were used to brace the building against wind.

In 1893 Corydon T. Purdy introduced rigid-frame design in the
Old Colony Building (Fig. 2.6). This was a narrow 16-storey building

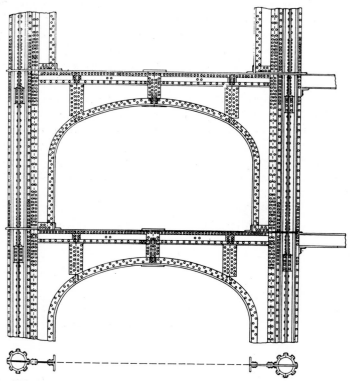

Fig. 2.6.   The steel frame of the Old Colony Building, erected in Chicago in
1893. A simply supported beam spanned the centre bay (visible on the right).
Rigid portal frames, one stacked above the other, were used in the outer bays.
The architects were Holabird and Roche, and the structural consultant was
Corydon T. Purdy. (From *Architectural Structures*, by J. K. Freitag. 2nd Edn.
Wiley, New York, 1901.)

exposed to wind on all four sides and it had large windows so that the walls could not be utilised for wind resistance. Purdy connected the steel girders in the outer bays to the columns with rivets through a deep rounded fillet. This produced a series of rigid portal frames (Section 3.8), capable of resisting wind forces, and stacked one above the other. This method was still used by H. G. Balcom in the 102-storey Empire State Building in 1929.

In Europe steel-framed buildings were not nearly as tall, and riveted connections made with angle cleats were normally used in the early 20th century. These connections were regarded as flexible for design of the frame to carry the vertical dead and live loads (Fig. 2.5). In designing for wind load it was assumed that the connections between the beams and the columns were sufficiently stiff to transmit bending moments, so that the frame deformed like the model in Fig. 3.8. Thus the curvature changed from convex to concave approximately half-way along the beams, and approximately half-way along the columns. Navier (Section 2.3) had already shown that at a point of contraflexure, that is, where the curvature changes from convex to concave, the bending moment is zero. A flexible joint could therefore be inserted at the point of contraflexure without changing the stress distribution. The frame can therefore be analysed by

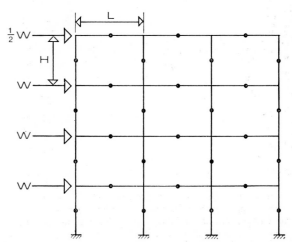

Fig. 2.7.   Design of small steel frame for wind load, assuming hypothetical flexible joints (or pin joints) at the points of contraflexure (Fig. 3.8).

assuming hypothetical flexible joints, or pin joints, at the points of contraflexure (Fig. 2.7). The frame then becomes statically determinate, that is, it can be solved by simple statics (Section 3.5).

Both these methods became obsolete when rigid frame analysis was developed (Section 3.8).

2.5. BUCKLING

Columns can fail in two entirely different ways. If a short column of steel is overloaded, the material is squashed out of shape, and it does not recover its original shape. The load at which failure occurs depends only on the yield stress of the material, that is, the stress at which it begins to deform visibly.

A column with a very high ratio of length to thickness, generally referred to as a 'long' column, shows an entirely different type of behaviour. On being overloaded it buckles; but the original shape is recovered on unloading. Its loadbearing capacity is, however, limited by its resistance to buckling (Fig. 2.8). The solution of the buckling failure was published by Leonard Euler in 1757 [67]. It is the oldest structural formula still in use today. Mathematically it is one of the most complicated problems in the elementary theory of structures. It shows that the buckling load depends only on the modulus of elasticity of the material and on the slenderness ratio of the column, *i.e.* the ratio of length to thickness. The buckling load is independent of the strength of the material. This means that a material with a low modulus of elasticity, like aluminium, is much more liable to buckling than steel. Metallurgical improvements in metals can greatly increase their strength, but they do not alter the modulus of elasticity, so that high-strength steel buckles at the same load as low-strength steel.

In fact iron and steel columns are neither so short as to fail purely by yielding, or so long as to fail purely by buckling; the actual failure involves both phenomena. Thus the Euler formula gives an answer which is too high, and therefore unsafe.

Tredgold [109] in 1824 published an empirical formula

$$P = fA/(1 + aL^2/d^2) \qquad (2.5)$$

where P is the working load for a circular column, f is the working

Fig. 2.8.   Elastic buckling failure of a 'long', *i.e.* a very slender, column. At a certain load, called the Euler load, the column suddenly deflects sideways and collapses. When the load is removed the column recovers its original shape. The column is not damaged by this elastic failure. The buckling load is greatly affected by the end supports of the column.

stress for the column, A is its cross-sectional area, L is its length, d is its diameter and a is a constant.

This formula, rephrased by Lewis Gordon, Professor of Engineering at Glasgow University, is still used in some building codes at the present time.

In 1858 Rankine, who had succeeded Gordon three years previously, provided a theoretical basis for eqn. (2.5). He argued that the working load for a short column, P_s, was correct for a ratio L/d of zero, and the working load for a 'long' or Euler column, P_e, was correct for a ratio L/d of infinity. For intermediate loads the working load of a column, P, could thus be obtained from

$$\frac{1}{P} = \frac{1}{P_s} + \frac{1}{P_e} \tag{2.6}$$

This gives the same answer as Tredgold's formula, if one determines the resulting constant by experiment.

In the 1880s two new column formulae were devised, based on the proposition that in practice columns are neither perfectly straight, nor perfectly concentrically loaded. Thus the load a column can carry is less than the Euler load for a perfectly straight column, perfectly concentrically loaded. R. H. Smith derived in 1887 the solution for a column whose load was slightly eccentric, and John Perry in 1886 derived the solution for a column with a slight initial curvature [68]. These formulae are now used in many building codes.

The effect of buckling is not limited to columns. In beams the crinkling of the compression flanges and of the web present serious problems. Many of the early failures of iron structures were due to these secondary effects. The first detailed study of this problem was made by William Fairbairn and Robert Stephenson during the construction of the two tubular bridges over the River Conway and the Menai Strait in Wales in 1845 [103]. These bridges consisted of thin-walled rectangular tubes through which the trains ran, as if in tunnels.

Cast iron was still more common for beams at that time than wrought iron, and cast iron beams, simply supported, failed by cracking on the tension face, because the strength of cast iron in tension was lower than in compression. Fairbairn noted (Section 4.1) that the wrought iron tubes failed on the compression side, and observed that this was 'totally different to anything yet exhibited in any previous research'. He reduced the working stresses on the compression face, and riveted stiffeners, in the form of iron angles, to the tubes to stop the crinkling. Both these devices are still used today in the design of steel girders built up from relatively thin plates.

2.6. The Rediscovery of Concrete

The origins of concrete construction, like those of so many other building techniques, can be traced back to Roman work carried out two thousand years ago. There were two types of Roman concrete. The first, called *opus signinum*, consisted of mortar with potsherds or with broken bricks. The second, called *opus caementitium*, consisted of mortar cast around large pieces of natural stone or rubble from the demolition of previous buildings. The first was used particularly for floors, and the second particularly for large structures. The word *caementum* denoted a piece of aggregate, not the cement.

The mortar in both cases consisted for ordinary work of lime and *fossiciae*, a term commonly translated as pit sand. This originated from extinct volcanoes in Italy, and it contained some alumina. Ordinary lime mortar, composed of a mixture of ordinary (*i.e.* silica) sand and lime, is water soluble, but, as the Roman mortar was resistant to water, it could therefore be used for waterproof or 'hydraulic' construction.

Vitruvius [11] recommended that when 'pit sand' was not available, and 'river sand' (that is, ordinary silica sand) had to be used, a third part of crushed earthenware should be added to the mortar. The alumina in the earthenware probably reacted slowly with the lime.

For work of the highest quality a volcanic ash was used with cementing properties stronger than those of 'pit sand'. There were several deposits; the best, *pulvis puteolanus* (pozzolana), which came from Putuoli, near Mount Vesuvius, was used in the Pantheon (Fig. 1.1).

The strength of Roman concrete is not much less than that of modern concrete. This relatively high strength may be partly due to age, and partly to good workmanship, but it probably owes more to a low water–cement ratio. Much of the *opus caementitium* was built with tufa, selce and other porous rocks of volcanic origin, or with broken brick, all of which absorb some water. Moreover, Pliny advised restraint in the use of water, and the mix was probably rather dry.

The Romans employed timber formwork, and the marks may still be seen, for example, on the Pantheon (Fig. 1.1). Use was made of hollow pots cast into the concrete to reduce the dead weight, as in a modern hollow-tile floor, for example in the tomb of Empress Helena near Rome. There are even a few instances of the use of metal bars (usually bronze) embedded in the concrete, for example in the roof of the Baths of Caracalla in Rome.

Waterproof concrete fell into disuse after the fall of the Roman Empire. During the Renaissance there was a revival of interest in

Roman concrete, as in all things Roman. Brunelleschi studied it, and Bramante stated that he used concrete in the ancient manner for the core of the piers of St Peter's in Rome. The reasons for the strength and waterproof character of Roman concrete were, however, not understood.

This was partly due to three statements made by Vitruvius [11], whose *Ten Books* had been treated with great respect since the 15th century. Vitruvius emphasised that very strong concrete could be made with pozzolana, which is correct; however, this volcanic ash had to be transported over long distances for use in Britain and France, and this made the material far too expensive for most purposes. The nearest deposits were found in the upper reaches of the River Rhine from where they were shipped *via* Holland under the name Rhenish trass.

Vitruvius wrote that the strongest lime was pure white and made from the hardest limestone. Both statements are wrong, but they were still repeated as late as 1753 by Bernard Forest de Belidor, a respected engineer, in *Architecture Hydraulique*. Vitruvius' prescription worked in Rome, because he specified the use of *fossiciae* (a sand which contained some alumina) or the addition of powdered brick, which was generally omitted in the 18th century.

The rediscovery of concrete was the result of a systematic investigation by John Smeaton [125] preceding the construction of the third Eddystone Lighthouse between 1756 and 1759. The Eddystone is a rock on the main shipping route from London to New York and Boston. One of the earliest lighthouses was built there in 1699 of timber, but this structure was destroyed by a spring tide in 1702. The second lighthouse, also of timber, was built in 1706 and destroyed by fire in 1755. Smeaton decided that it was necessary to build a lighthouse of stone, using mortar which, unlike lime mortar, was water-resistant.

He experimented with lime from various deposits, and disproved Belidor's rule that the strongest limestone made the strongest lime. Mortar made from soft white chalk had the same strength as mortar made from the hardest white marble. He then observed that the strongest mortars were not produced by the whitest limes. He made a particularly strong mortar with lime produced from a bluish limestone from Aberthaw in Wales. He dissolved this rock in *aqua fortis* (concentrated nitric acid), and obtained an insoluble deposit which he identified as clay; this amounted to one eighth of the original weight. He concluded that water-resistant lime mortar needed to be made from a limestone which contained a reasonable proportion of clay, and he pointed out that there were many deposits in England which could be used to produce water-resistant lime mortar.

In 1796 James Parker produced a natural cement (*i.e.* a cement made from a naturally occurring single deposit) from 'stones of clay containing calcareous matter' found near London.

Smeaton had made his lime in the traditional manner, by burning the limestone ($CaCO_3$) to produce quicklime (CaO) and then slaking this with water. He thus used only sufficient heat to drive off the carbon dioxide from the calcium carbonate. Parker used a much higher temperature, and then ground the product into a powder which he called 'Roman cement'. Actually the material was quite different from Roman cement, but Roman concrete still had a great reputation. In 1796 the first natural cement was produced in France, and in 1818 in America. Natural cement remained an important material throughout the 19th century, and even in 1850 it was preferred by many architects and engineers to portland cement [119 and 120].

The first artificial cement (*i.e.* a cement made from two different materials) was made by Joseph Aspden in 1811. He used finely divided clay and limestone, mixed them together, burnt them and ground the resulting clinker. He called it portland cement, a name probably inspired by Smeaton's book on the Eddystone Lighthouse [125]. Smeaton had said that the cement he had made from Aberthaw limestone was 'equivalent to the best commercially obtainable Portland stone for strength and durability'. The grey portland cement looks quite different from the white Portland stone, a fine-grained limestone used for the Eddystone Lighthouse and also for some of the most important buildings erected in London during the 18th and 19th centuries. However, the name had good advertising value, and well-made portland cement concrete is indeed as strong and as durable as Portland stone, if rather unattractive in appearance by comparison.

Parker's cement depended on limited deposits of naturally pre-mixed material. Portland cement is made by burning together finely divided limestone and clay (or shale), and it can be made almost anywhere. The first factories for portland cement outside Britain were opened in France in 1840, in Germany in 1855, in the USA in 1871 and in Australia in 1889.

Plain concrete was used extensively as a structural material in public works during the 19th century, including bridges spanning over 60 m (197 ft) [151].

In building construction concrete was used as infilling over brick jack arches to form the floors of industrial buildings (Fig. 2.1).

In 1812 John Nash employed Parker's Roman cement for the stucco of Park Crescent in London. London had grown in the 17th and 18th century, and new squares were laid out in a uniform style and material. Portland and Bath stone were employed for the best squares, but the cheaper brick was used elsewhere. In the late 18th century there was a search for a new form of construction which looked like stone, but cost only as much as brick. Robert Adam had used stucco in Hanover Square in 1776, but the use of waterproof cement greatly improved the durability.

A few complete houses of plain concrete were built in England and in France in the 1830s, but concrete was rarely used as the principal building material prior to the introduction of reinforcement.

2.7. The Beginnings of Reinforced Concrete Construction

In the 1850s a number of patents for reinforcing concrete were registered in England, but the only one known to have been used was that filed in 1854 by William Boutland Wilkinson [121]. He erected a number of buildings in Newcastle upon Tyne, using old wire rope obtained from the mines together with small iron bars as reinforcement. Although he lived to the age of 83 and his successful building form survived him, his impact on reinforced concrete design was slight.

In 1855 Joseph Louis Lambot exhibited a boat, patented earlier that year, made from cement mortar and iron bars, at the Paris Universal Exhibition.

In the same year François Coignet patented a method of concrete floor construction with some reinforcement. In 1862 Coignet built himself in St Denis, a suburb of Paris, a three-storey residence with mouldings in the style of Palladio. It was entirely of concrete, and the floors were reinforced with iron I-beams. François Coignet was ruined by the economic collapse which followed the fall of Paris to the Germans in 1871, but his son Edmond later carried on a successful business as a reinforced concrete designer.

In 1863 Joseph Monier patented a reinforced concrete flower pot. Monier was, like Joseph Paxton (Section 6.6) interested in the layout of gardens, and he needed the large pots for growing trees in green-houses. In 1873 he took out an additional patent for constructing beams and vaults in reinforced concrete. In 1879 Gustav Adolf Wayss acquired the German rights to the Monier System [118].

The American development was essentially separate. Thaddeus Hyatt undertook the first experimental work on reinforced concrete in 1855. In 1866 Ernest Leslie Ransome arrived in the USA from England to work in a factory making precast concrete blocks, and he soon started to branch out into reinforced concrete. In 1884 he patented spiral-twisted square bars to improve the concrete bond. His first important building was a three-storey museum built in 1889 at the newly established Stanford University, near San Francisco. It has reinforced concrete walls, a reinforced concrete floor paved with marble, concrete tiles on interlocking iron trusses, and iron windows to make a completely fireproof building. The concrete facade is classical, and the concrete finish is exceptionally good for its time. Ransome removed the cement film by tooling and exposed the aggregate.

In 1902 Ransome built the first concrete skyscraper, the 16-storey Ingalls Building in Cincinatti. This had a skeleton frame and the walls did not bear any load.

During this time Britain relied mainly on foreign inventions for reinforced concrete. By the end of the 19th century 43 different patent systems were in use [127]; of these 15 were originally patented in France, 14 in Germany or Austria-Hungary, and 8 in the United States. Some employed complex and highly original systems of reinforcement, in others the arrangement of the reinforcement was similar to that in use today (Fig. 2.9). In the end, the simplest arrangements of the reinforcement proved as effective as the more complicated systems and they were more economical in labour.

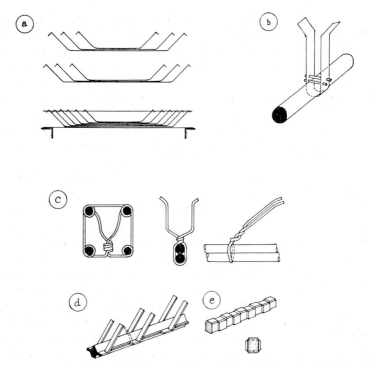

Fig. 2.9. Some patented reinforcing systems used in Britain at the beginning of the 20th century: (a) Coignet bent-up bars (French); (b) Hennebique stirrups (French); (c) BRC hooping and stirrups (British); (d) Kahn bar (American); (e) Indented bar (British) [127].

In 1885 Mattias Koenen, the chief engineer of the firm Wayss and Freytag, wrote a book *Das System Monier*, published by the company, which contained the first theory of reinforced concrete design. Koenen proposed that Hooke's Law should be assumed to apply to the concrete as well as to the iron, that the iron should be assumed to resist the whole of the tension, and that perfect adhesion should be assumed between the iron and the concrete. Koenen, however, did not know how to determine the depth of the neutral axis and placed it half-way down the section. This mistake was corrected by Edmond Coignet in a paper read before the Société des Ingénieurs Civils de France in 1894.

This elastic theory remained the basis of reinforced concrete design until the 1950s (Section 3.9). It was used in the first course on reinforced concrete, given at the École des Ponts et Chaussées in Paris in 1897, and by Paul Christophe in the first textbook *Le Béton Armé et ses Applications*, published in Liège (Belgium) in 1899. Charles F. Marsh used the same method in the first English-language book [127] in 1904.

Koenen was also the first to point out that the coefficient of thermal expansion of iron and of concrete was nearly the same, so that no internal stresses would be set up between the iron and the concrete due to changes in temperature; this is an essential requirement for a fireproof material.

The firm of Wayss and Freytag financed the first research programme on the behaviour of reinforced concrete. This was undertaken at the Technische Hochschule in Stuttgart by Professor Carl von Bach and Dr Otto Graf. It was a very thorough investigation, even by present-day standards. By 1914 the main principles had been established. There are four ways in which a simply supported reinforced concrete beam can fail. One is through gradual yielding of the reinforcement which causes the neutral axis to rise (Fig. 2.10(a)) until the concrete on top is crushed and the beam collapses. This takes time, and this type of failure therefore gives warning of impending collapse; beams are normally designed to fail in this manner. The second is through crushing of concrete on top while the beam is still elastic (Fig. 2.10(b)). This occurs suddenly, and as there is little warning, it is a type of failure to be avoided. The third type of failure is caused by shear which produces a diagonal tension crack (Fig. 2.10(c)). This can be delayed, but not entirely avoided by shear reinforcement. Fourthly, failure can occur because the reinforcement is not adequately bonded and anchored to the concrete. In the early 20th century this was prevented by using hooks at the ends of the bars, but it is now customary to use deformed bars and hooks are rarely needed.

Reinforced concrete being composed of two materials, the mathematics of its theory is more complex than for a single material. However, the principle is essentially simple, and the apparent complexity of the equations is superficial and not important in practice.

The solution has been greatly simplified by design charts and

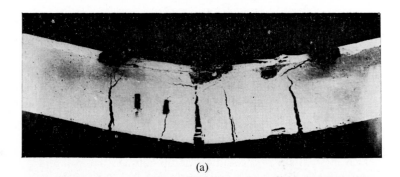

(a)

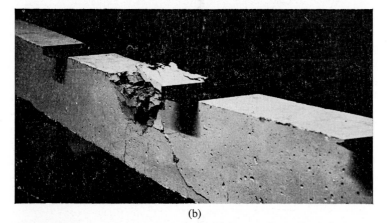

(b)

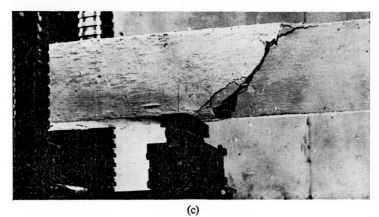

(c)

tables. Although the designer's task is not as simple as in the case of structural steel, this is mainly due to the difficulty of standardising reinforced concrete sections.

The ability to vary reinforced concrete freely to suit the architectural requirements of the building is also one of its great advantages, since it allows the designer to decide on a size of concrete section desirable from aesthetic and planning considerations, or the requirements of the other constructional details, and then provide the requisite strength by suitable reinforcement. In addition, reinforced concrete provides the body as well as the skeleton of the building.

The assessment of the strength of reinforced concrete sections is therefore not the main problem posed by the reinforced concrete and frame building; the real difficulty arises from the continuity of the structure. Since the beams and the columns are normally cast in one piece, bending moments are transmitted from each beam to the adjacent beams and also to the columns.

In the late 19th and early 20th century this problem was solved by empirical moment coefficients relating the load acting on the beam to the maximum bending moment produced by it. This method, devised by François Hennebique, and still widely in use, has the undoubted merit of simplicity; however, it greatly limits the designer. In view of the complexity and importance of this problem, it is not surprising that it gave rise to a vast number of books and technical papers (Section 3.8). Eventually the digital computer provided the means of obtaining an economical and accurate solution (Section 4.3).

Fig. 2.10.   Failure of simply supported reinforced concrete beams: (a) When there is a small amount of tension reinforcement, by initial yielding of the steel. This is followed by a gradual rise in the neutral axis, and by crushing of the concrete. The beam then collapses. (b) When there is a large amount of tension reinforcement, by crushing of the concrete while the steel is still elastic. The beam collapses immediately. (c) By shear, which produces a diagonal tension crack.

Chapter 3

Two-Dimensional Structures, and the Development of the Rigid Frame Theory

You must learn to think as the structure thinks.

Hardy Cross

3.1. TIMBER TRUSSES AND STEEL TRUSSES

Beams and lintels have evident limitations for long spans; depth is needed to carry loads across a considerable distance, and this can only be achieved by the use of deep beams which are heavy and extravagant in the use of material (Fig. 4.6), by arches which exert a horizontal thrust difficult to accommodate at a great height above the ground, or else by trusses.

Although few old timber structures survive, they are properly the forerunners of modern structural techniques. Timber roofs, similar to those used in modern domestic construction, have been built from the very earliest times. The Romans built timber structures of longer span, although none survives. Trojan's Column in Rome, for example, shows a bridge with a wooden superstructure built by Apollodorus of Damascus across the Danube in Rumania [86]. Caesar in his book on the Gallic wars described in detail a wooden bridge which he built over the Rhine, and Palladio [15] made a drawing from this description.

Large triangulated timber trusses were revived during the Renaissance by Palladio, who built several bridges exceeding 30 m (98 ft) in span (Fig. 3.1). Records of old timber bridges are necessarily incomplete, but it is evident that the 19th century could look back on a long tradition of timber bridge truss construction.

Since the theory of the statically determinate truss is one of the simplest problems in structural mechanics, and all the elements for a solution were available in the 16th century, it is surprising that no serious attempt towards scientific design was made before the 19th century. The impetus was provided by the needs of the railways, whose construction commenced in 1821. The entire problem was solved between 1840 and 1870.

The building of the railways posed a new problem because of the number and the size of the bridges required in a very short time. The railway train is incapable of negotiating steep gradients uphill or downhill, nor can it operate until the permanent way is complete.

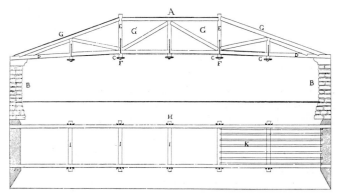

Fig. 3.1. Bridge built by Andrea Palladio over the River Cimone. Palladio built this 30 m (98 ft) bridge in one span because the current was so strong that an intermediate support would have been swept away. In the *Four Books* he defined the diagonal members as 'the arms, which bearing contrary to each other, support the whole work'. (Ref. 15, page 65.)

In western Europe, where the first railways were built in densely populated areas, the bridges were mostly built with brick or stone arches, and considerable emphasis was placed on the need for the engineering work to blend with the landscape.

In America and in Russia the sparse population and the long distances enforced economy in initial expenditure, and timber trusses were used during the early years. Howe's trusses, still known by his name, were similar to Palladio's, except that iron was substituted for the tension members; this reduced the weight and eliminated some of the expensive timber-to-timber joints. Because of the danger of fire, bridges of the same type were built after 1840 entirely in wrought iron, and the cost of the material made scientific methods of design imperative. Failures were not uncommon, although they were probably due mainly to inadequate bracing or to buckling of the compression members [68].

3.2. THE THEORY OF STATICALLY DETERMINATE STRUCTURES

The first analysis of the truss was given by Squire Whipple, an American bridge builder from Utica, NY, in 1847, and independently by D. I. Jourawski, a Russian railway engineer, in 1850. This is now called the Method of Resolution of the Joints; the forces in the members are obtained by considering the conditions of equilibrium at each joint in turn. This method relies entirely on calculations.

In 1862 the German engineer A. Ritter produced another analytical approach, the Method of Sections. Ritter cut the truss along an imaginary line, and replaced the internal forces by equivalent external forces. By making a sufficient number of cuts and taking moments about convenient points the magnitude of the forces can be obtained.

The third method was the most useful in the mid-19th century, because it used graphics instead of calculations. A good draughtsman working on a large drawing board (known as double elephant size) could obtain an accurate result far more quickly with a geometric construction than with arithmetic. Logarithmic tables were freely available, but the mid-19th century slide rule (Section 4.3) had no cursor and it was not very accurate. Gaspard Monge, the founder of the École Polytechnique (Section 2.1) in Paris, encouraged graphic methods wherever they could be used.

Graphic statics was developed independently by Clerk Maxwell, at that time Professor of Physics and Astronomy at King's College, London, and best known for his work on electromagnetism, and by Karl Culmann, Professor of Engineering Science at the newly founded Eidgenössische Technische Hochschule in Zurich. Maxwell published his work first, in 1864, in the *Philosophical Magazine* which few engineers read. It became known only when Robert Bow included it in 1873 in his book *Economics of Construction*. He introduced the notation which still bears his name (Fig. 3.2).

The three principal methods for the analysis of plane trusses were therefore developed in a period of less than twenty years, after centuries of truss design by empirical methods. It demonstrates how an urgent need can act as a stimulus.

All these theories are based on the assumption that the members of a truss are pin-jointed. The early trusses were, in fact, connected

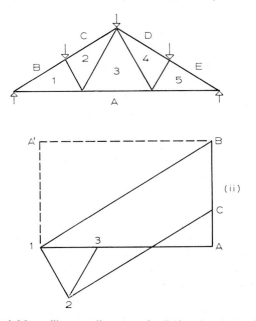

Fig. 3.2. Clerk Maxwell's stress diagram, using Robert Bow's notation in which the spaces between the members, not the joints, are lettered and numbered. Each joint is in equilibrium since the truss does not move. Considering the joint at the left-hand support, the external force AB is known, and it can be drawn to a suitable scale (for example, 1 kN = 1 mm). The internal force in the member A1 is horizontal, and the internal force in the member B1 is parallel to that member. The intersection of these two lines gives the location of the point 1 on the stress diagram (ii). (The dotted line B A′ 1 completes the parallelogram of forces.) Each joint is considered in turn, until the complete compound stress diagram (ii) is produced. The internal forces are then measured using the scale of the diagram.

in this manner. For example, the truss patented in England by James Warren in 1848, and still known by his name, originally consisted of cast iron compression members, with holes for the pins embodied in the casting, and wrought iron tie bars forged to form eyes at the ends, the members being connected by pins and cotters. The pinned connections were in time replaced by riveted, bolted or welded joints, which no longer permitted free rotation of the members. However, if the members are sufficiently flexible to permit the requisite deformation of the truss, the disturbance is mainly in the vicinity of the joint, and it is normal practice to treat trusses as 'pinned' unless the connections are unusually rigid.

3.3. CONDITIONS FOR STATICAL DETERMINATENESS

The simplest plane frame consists of three pin-jointed members. If extra joints are to be added to this elementary frame, two additional members are required for each extra pin. This problem was considered in 1837 by Ferdinand Möbius, Professor of Astronomy at the University of Leipzig, who included in his *Lehrbuch der Statik* (Textbook of statics) the formula

$$n = 2j - 3 \qquad (3.1)$$

where n is the number of members in a truss, and j is the number of joints.

If fewer members are used, the frame can be deformed by the slightest load; it is in fact a mechanism and not a structure. If more members are used, the structure becomes more rigid; but there are more forces than can be determined by the simple laws of statics, and the structure becomes statically indeterminate. In order to obtain a solution, it is necessary to consider in addition to the statical equilibrium either the elastic deformation of the frame (elastic design), or else its mode of collapse (ultimate strength design). The amount of work involved depends mainly on the number of redundant members, *i.e.* members which are additional to those required for a statically determinate structure (Section 3.5). For a large number of redundant members the amount of work is very considerable (Chapter 4).

Since the statically determinate structure is a mechanism with one additional member, this last member is bound to fit. If the setting out is slightly inaccurate it is still possible to assemble the frame without undue force; although the frame would not be quite true to shape, this may not be a serious matter.

In a statically indeterminate frame the redundant members must be exactly true if they are to be fitted without force. This is particularly difficult in large precast concrete frames, for which a statically determinate design is more satisfactory in practice.

3.4. Prestressing

On the other hand, it may be advantageous to introduce deliberately members which are too long or too short, and force them into position with a hydraulic jack or a turnbuckle, as the case may be. The frame is then stressed before any load is applied; if these stresses are mainly opposite to those produced by the load, the load carrying capacity of the structure is increased. This form of prestressing was used in many of the early trusses on an empirical basis. Today it is not uncommon to prestress a cable between the supports of a long-span roof. This lifts the structure off its formwork and thus serves a double purpose: it simplifies the removal of the formwork, and it improves stress distribution in the structure by opposing the stresses due to its weight (Section 4.6), Since the structure begins to carry its own weight as soon as it lifts off the formwork, the stress due to the weight of the structure and the prestress may each be in excess of the permissible stress, provided that the combined stress due to both is within the permissible range.

While prestressing has occasionally been used in steel structures, its main advantage is in conjunction with concrete, which is much stronger in compression than in tension. By superimposing an appropriate eccentric compression it is possible to remove the tensile stresses due to bending and so obtain a structure free from the haircracks which inevitably occur in normal reinforced concrete. This was realised as early as 1886, when C. W. F. Doehring, in Germany, patented a method for the manufacture of mortar slabs with steel-wire reinforcement. Almost as old is P. H. Jackson's American patent (1888) for inducing preliminary compressive stresses in concrete arches and floor structures by tightening tie rods with the aid of turnbuckles [142].

All the 19th century attempts to prestress concrete failed. The prestress disappeared almost entirely after a period of time because it was too low and the time-dependent deformation of concrete (shrinkage and creep) had not been allowed for.

When concrete hardens, some of the water with which the dry components are mixed is lost by evaporation, and some combines chemically with the cement. As a result the concrete shrinks by approximately 0·03%. This causes a contraction in the prestressing steel, and a change in the length of the steel of 0·03% producing a change in stress of approximately 60 MPa (10 ksi), more than half the stress admissible in 19th-century reinforcing steels. More than half the prestress is thus dissipated by shrinkage alone. There is a further loss due to creep, the time-dependent deformation of concrete first observed in 1907 by W. K. Hatt. The prestressing force acting over long periods squeezes water out of the pores of the material, with consequent contraction of the concrete and the prestressing steel, and a further loss of prestress.

Eugène Freyssinet first appreciated this problem in the 1920s and began experiments with concrete of very high strength prestressed with piano wire. Using prestresses ten times as great as that of Doehring, he reduced the loss to a little over 10%. The use of high-tensile steel is thus a necessity for prestressed concrete.

Steel with the high strength suitable for prestressing cannot be employed in normal reinforced concrete. The concrete extends with the steel and the cracks become excessive when the steel stress exceeds about 200 MPa (30 ksi). This limitation does not apply to prestressed concrete which is designed to be free from cracks, so that there is no upper limit to the permissible steel stress apart from that imposed by the potentialities of steel production. It is therefore possible to supply the resultant tensile force in the section with a much smaller cross-sectional area of steel, and the resulting steel economy was the principal reason for the rapid development of prestressed concrete immediately after World War II when steel was in short supply. Many new methods were patented [143], as in the early days of reinforced concrete.

At present this economy in the use of steel and concrete is not sufficient to compensate for the high cost of prestressing, when the spans are comparatively short as in buildings, thus most of the applications of prestressed concrete are in bridge construction.

However, for shell structures prestressing has the added advantage that it lifts the structure off the formwork (Section 4.6).

3.5. ADVANTAGES AND DISADVANTAGES OF STATICALLY INDETERMINATE STRUCTURES

Any statically determinate structure can be made statically indeterminate by introducing stiff joints, additional members, or additional reactions. The reverse process can be achieved by introducing additional pin joints.

An additional support or an additional member adds a redundancy. A rigid joint, for example a joint in a cast-in-place concrete structure or a joint in a steel structure stiffened with a substantial cleat, also adds a redundancy to the frame. The introduction of an extra pin, on the other hand, removes a redundancy (Fig. 3.3).

The early long-span steel structures were almost invariably statically determinate, because their theory was clearly understood. The statically determinate version of the beam continuous over a number of supports is the cantilever girder, which was first employed on a grand scale in the Firth of Forth Bridge (Fig. 3.4), to this day one of the masterpieces of bridge building. By introducing two pins into the span which supports a short girder, the beam is rendered statically determinate. This method has been used in recent years in precast concrete, where the 'pin' can be produced cheaply by a scarf joint which permits the requisite rotation.

The statically determinate version of the rigid frame is the three-pin portal. There being no bending moment at the top pin, the horizontal reaction can be determined by taking moments about this pin, and the vertical reactions are obtained in the usual way. The Galerie des Machines, built for the Paris International Exhibition of 1889, consisted of a series of three-pinned portals (Section 2.2), which introduced a new aesthetic into the design of buildings. The art historian Siegfried Giedion contrasted them with the traditional stone vaults: 'Moving downward, the trusses become increasingly attenuated until they appear scarcely to touch the ground; moving upwards, they spread and gain weight and power. The usual proportions seem to be exactly reversed. These truly articulated arches

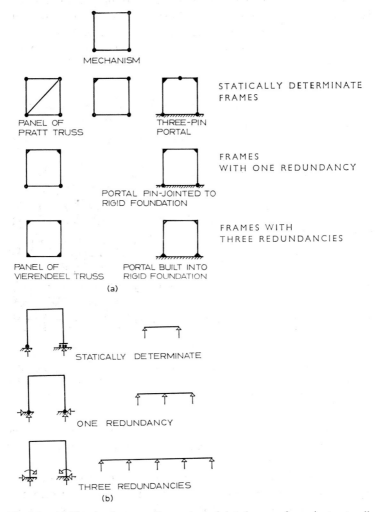

Fig. 3.3.   (a) The simple square frame. A pin-jointed square frame is structurally unstable. It can be rendered statically determinate by two rigid joints together with a pin joint. A rigidly jointed square panel has three redundancies. (b) Comparison of portal frames with a continuous beam. The effect of adding an additional rigid joint is the same as that of adding an additional reaction.

disturb, or rather disrupt, traditional static feelings with regard to the rational relations of support and load. Elongated like immensely drawn-out cantilevers, the trusses embody movement in all their parts. Nothing remains of the quiet stone architecture of the barrel vault.' (Ref. 101, page 271.)

Fig. 3.4.   The Firth of Forth Bridge, north of Edinburgh, commenced in 1883 and completed in 1890. The designer of the bridge, Sir Benjamin Baker, at a public lecture demonstrated its structural principle with a living model consisting of two men whose linked arms supported a boy. The men represented two of the cantilever spans, and the boy represented the inset span between them [87].

In the 20th century Robert Maillart [137] utilised the same principle in a number of bridges set in spectacular scenery in the Swiss Alps (Fig. 3.5).

The choice between the statically determinate and the statically indeterminate structure depends on a number of factors. The removal of a single member turns a statically determinate structure into a mechanism so that it collapses. The statically indeterminate structure has therefore, by its very nature, a greater margin of safety. Only when all the redundancies have been removed by the formation of hinges, and one further additional hinge has formed, can the structure collapse. This collapse mechanism is utilised in the plastic theory for structural design (Section 3.9). Rigid frames are thus stronger for the same amount of material and they provide a greater margin of safety against accidental damage by internal explosions, for example from domestic gas appliances [175 and 176], against collapse when the structure is weakened by a severe fire and against earthquakes [173 and 174].

Fig. 3.5. The characteristic shape of Maillart's reinforced concrete bridges results from the junction of the road slab with the three-pin arch at the point where the bending moment in the arch, and consequently the depth required, reaches its maximum. This produces a massive concrete structure which blends with the great mountains forming the background.

On the other hand, the members of a statically determinate structure fit even if slightly oversized or undersized; changes in dimensions due to temperature or moisture movement can be absorbed without causing additional stresses, and stresses due to uneven settlement are avoided.

3.6. Continuity: The Design of Reinforced Concrete Frames

The Firth of Forth Bridge and the Galerie des Machines, in spite of their great span, were basically simple structures. Their impressiveness was due largely to the clear expression of the structure. The structural behaviour of the ordinary skeleton frame building is much more complex, but in the 19th and early 20th century it was generally assumed that the steel skeleton was statically determinate. The riveted or bolted connections were relatively flexible, and if wind load could be ignored, the columns were then considered to be cantilevering from the ground, with the beams simply supported between them (Fig. 2.5).

This simple picture is unsatisfactory for reinforced concrete, which requires steel on the tension face, but not on the compression face. In a steel frame a reversal in bending moment from positive (compression on top, tension at the bottom) to negative (tension at the top) is not serious, provided the bending moments are not at the limit of the permissible stresses. In reinforced concrete structures it is important to provide steel on the tension face, however small the bending moments.

The slabs and beams in the earliest reinforced concrete frames were designed on the assumption that they were restrained at the ends. The theory of beams fully restrained or 'built-in', at their supports was solved by Navier in his *Résumé des leçons* (Section 2.3) in 1826. He noted that if the beam was built in, its supports could not rotate at all, and that the slope at the supports was therefore zero. A simply supported beam deflects downwards, so that there is a downward slope at the ends. This is prevented by building the beam into the end supports, which thus produce restraining moments which, if they acted by themselves, could cause the beam to deflect upwards. Thus the end slope due to the load acting on the simply supported beam is exactly equal and opposite to the end slope due to the restraining moments. The restraining moments cannot be determined by statics, *i.e.* they are statically indeterminate. However, they enable us to make a geometric statement, namely that the end slope is zero, and this produced the additional equation needed to solve the problem (Fig. 3.6).

Hennebique (Section 2.7) introduced in the 1890s empirical bending moment coefficients, derived from the theory of built-in beams, for the design of reinforced concrete skeleton frames. In the 1910s the theory of continuous beams was being adapted to the design of reinforced concrete frames.

Whereas steel frames generally consisted only of the columns and the beams, reinforced concrete floor slabs were usually cast in one piece with the floor beams. The floor structure was therefore much stiffer than the columns, and it could be regarded, as a first approximation, to be continuous over the more flexible columns.

The theory of continuous beams had been derived by B. P. E. Clapeyron in France in 1849. Six years later H. Bertot expressed it in terms of the moments in two adjacent spans, and in this convenient

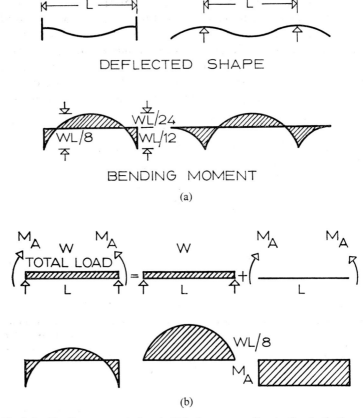

Fig. 3.6. Bending moments in a built-in beam according to the elastic theory. (a) Since the beam is rigidly restrained by its supports, its deflected shape must conform to those restraints, *i.e.* the slope at the supports is zero. The supports impose restraining moments on the beam which are superimposed on the bending moment due to the vertical load. The beam therefore behaves in the same way as the central portion of a simply supported beam with cantilever overhangs which are just long enough to keep the beam horizontal at its supports. (b) The bending moment diagram is therefore composed of two parts: the usual bending moment diagram for a simply supported beam, and a uniform restraining moment M_A. It can be shown that the area of these two bending moment diagrams is equal, so that the net bending moment at the supports

$$M_A = \frac{2}{3}\frac{WL}{8} = \frac{WL}{12}$$

This is also the maximum bending moment in the beam.

form it has become known as the Theorem of Three Moments (Fig. 3.7). This became the principal method for the design of reinforced concrete skeleton frames. The slabs were generally designed by empirical coefficients, the beams were considered continuous over the columns, and a proportion of the bending moments at the junction between the beams and the columns was considered to be transmitted to the columns, which were designed to withstand these bending moments.

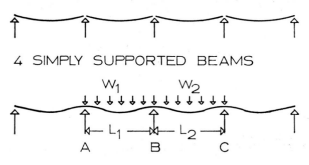

Fig. 3.7.   Simply supported beam and continuous beam. Four simply supported beams deflect independently, whereas a beam continuous over four spans deflects to form a continuous curve. Considering the two central spans of the continuous beam, it can be shown that the restraining moments at the supports A, B and C are related by the Theorem of Three Moments

$$M_A L_1 + 2M_B(L_1 + L_2) + M_C L_2 = -\tfrac{1}{4}(W_1 L_1{}^2 + W_2 L_2{}^2)$$

One of these equations can be set up for each pair of adjacent spans, so that the geometric statement of continuity of deflections provides as many equations as there are unknown intermediate supports.

3.7. TWO-WAY ACTION IN CONCRETE FLOORS

The traditional timber-framed multi-storey building consisted of timber columns which carried primary timber beams or girders; these supported secondary timber beams or joists, which in turn carried timber planks at right angles to the joists and parallel to the girders. Each structural member was thus spanning in one direction, at right angles to the members which supported it.

The iron-framed and later the steel-framed building behaved in precisely the same way, except that the floor was generally formed of a different material, such as timber planks or brick arches, or later reinforced concrete slabs. The earliest reinforced concrete skeleton frames were also designed on the same principle.

However, in the late 19th century it was realised that a reinforced concrete slab in fact bent in two directions at right angles to one another. This is easily demonstrated by loading a flexible sheet, for example of foam rubber, supported on its four edges. Each unit square of the slab could therefore be regarded as forming part of two unit strips spanning at right angles to one another. Each of these strips carried a part of the load, and wherever they intersected they had the same deflection. This gave the additional equations for determining how much of the total load was carried in each direction. The reinforcement required in the two directions at right angles to one another could thus be calculated. Formulae for the design of *two-way slabs* based in this consideration first appeared in building codes in the decade following 1900 [131].

In the same decade beamless concrete floors came into use. Without supporting beams the column is liable to punch through the concrete slab, and the earliest beamless reinforced concrete slabs therefore had enlarged column heads. The first patent for *a flat slab* was taken out by Orlando Norcross in the USA, in 1902, but the subsequent development of the flat slab was mainly due to C. A. P. Turner [132]. Turner claimed to have built by 1914 flat-slab structures worth 200 million dollars. The flat slab was developed independently by Robert Maillart, but Maillart did not build his first flat-slab structure until 1912 [137].

The enlarged column heads are a prominent feature of the flat slabs, and for this reason they were also called 'mushroom floors'. Maillart's mushrooms gradually curved into the slab which made them look more elegant, but the cheaper straight column heads used in America became the normal practice.

In 1878 F. Grashof, Professor of Applied Mechanics at the Technische Hochschule in Karlsruhe, had derived an elastic solution for the firebox of a steam locomotive, in which the boiler plate was connected at right angles to a number of steam pipes. This was basically the same problem as that of a concrete slab supported at right angles by a number of columns. In 1917 Grashof's theory, with empirical modifications, was adopted in America for the design of flat slabs [124]; it was later replaced by a more accurate elastic analysis due to H. M. Westergaard [133], again with empirical modifications.

In 1933 the *equivalent-frame* method was introduced in California for the design of flat slabs. The flat slabs and their supporting columns were treated as a series of elastic frames (Section 3.8) interacting at right angles.

The enlarged column heads were first omitted by Joseph Di Stasio [134] in 1940. In order to distinguish the slab with column capitals from the slab without column capitals, the latter is now called a *flat plate*.

The flat plate represents the ultimate in structural simplicity, since it consists merely of concrete plates of uniform thickness and of columns of uniform section. It requires more concrete, but the formwork is cheap and so is the placing of the reinforcement and of the concrete. The omission of the enlarged column head reduces the area resisting the punching shear around the column, but the column can be made a little larger than is otherwise required, and the spans of flat plates are usually modest.

3.8. THE ELASTIC THEORY OF RIGID FRAMES

The first effective method for the design of rigid frames was given by Alberto Castigliano in 1873. It was a remarkable achievement since he presented it as a thesis for his degree to the Turin Politecnico at the age of 26. His work had little influence in his time, partly perhaps because he died when only 37 years old, partly also because steel and reinforced concrete were not yet normal structural materials. The examples in Castigliano's book, published in French in 1879 [82], deal with structures built from cast iron and wrought iron.

Castigliano determined the *strain energy*, or total energy stored in the body due to its elastic deformation, and then employed the Principle of Least Work to examine the conditions which made this energy a minimum. Since the differential coefficient of a function is zero when that function passes through a minimum, this procedure gives one equation for each statically indeterminate member of the frame. The method is satisfactory when there are only a few statically indeterminate members, but it is too cumbersome for the rigid skeleton of a multi-storey building. It remains, however, a good method for curved members, for example, rigid arches.

The problem can also be approached, as in the Theorem of Three Moments, by considering the deformation of the structure. If it is assumed that each right-angled stiff joint remains a right angle after the frame has been deformed by the loads acting on it, the change in slope of any two members terminating at the same joint must be the same (Fig. 3.8). By this process a series of simultaneous equations

Fig. 3.8.   Model of an elastic multi-storey frame with rigid joints, deformed by a horizontal force. It is assumed that the joints are sufficiently rigid to ensure that the right angles at the joints remain right angles, however much the rest of the frame deforms. Approximately half-way along the beams and half-way along the columns the curvature changes from convex to concave. At these *points of contraflexure* the bending moment is zero.

are obtained, from which the statically indeterminate members can be determined. This approach was originally proposed by Professor Otto Mohr at the Dresden Polytechnikum in 1892. In its present form it was published independently by A. Bendixen in Germany in 1914, and G. A. Maney in the United States in 1915 [84].

Maney demonstrated the potentialities of *slope-deflection analysis* by working out a complete multi-storey frame. This was a prodigious feat without modern calculating machinery, but it also demonstrated that the method, although simpler than Castigliano's, was still unsuitable for tall multi-bay frames, because of the large number of simultaneous equations.

Due to the laborious character of these methods, the moments and forces in the majority of rigid frames during the 1920s and 1930s were determined by semi-empirical methods, frequently standardised by a rule in a code of practice or building by-law. The dimensions of the sections were then calculated accurately from these approximate bending moments. One of the dangers of this procedure is the illusion of accuracy created in the mind of the designer by the precision of the second part, which can be no more accurate than the empirical bending moment coefficient. Nevertheless, the method worked well for conventional frames of limited height.

The efforts made in the 1930s to produce more accurate design processes took three main forms.

The bending moments were tabulated for a number of standard frames, notably by Adolf Kleinlogel, Professor of Concrete Structures at the Technische Hochschule in Darmstadt, Germany. While it is a simple matter to tabulate all conceivable loading conditions for continuous beams and for single-bay portals and arches, the possible combinations for multi-bay frames are, however, too numerous.

In 1930 Hardy Cross, Professor of Structural Engineering at the University of Illinois, proposed the *Moment Distribution Method* [83]. Like the slope-deflection analysis it was based on the assumption that a right-angle rigid joint remained a right angle after the structure had deformed.

Initially all the joints of the frame are assumed firmly clamped. The beams and the columns are therefore assumed built-in at the ends and the moments in them are determined accordingly from the standard equations. At most joints this clamping produces unbalanced moments. In a rectangular frame carrying vertical loads, for example, there are substantial moments in the beams and no moments in the columns. Each of the joints is then released in turn, and the unbalanced moment is distributed to the adjoining members. The process of releasing the joints in turn and distributing the moments can be continued indefinitely, and the unbalanced moments become smaller and smaller. In practice, however, a sufficient degree of accuracy is frequently obtained with three distributions, and two may be satisfactory for a preliminary design. The procedure need not, therefore, be laborious, and it is possible to adjust the amount of work to the importance of the problem. Moreover, Cross's method can be learned by persons with only limited mathematical knowledge. As a result many consulting engineers accepted it as a standard design procedure, whereas the strain-energy and slope-deflection methods had only been used for major structural problems.

The arithmetical computation involved in the analysis of a complete multi-storey rigid frame by moment distribution would be excessive without a digital computer (Section 4.3). However, the moments distributed from any one storey to the adjacent storeys have only a slight effect further away. It is therefore sufficiently accurate to consider each floor in turn together with the adjacent columns, assumed to be rigidly restrained at their remote ends (Fig. 3.9).

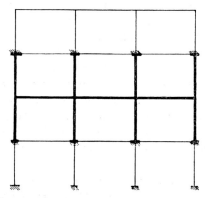

Fig. 3.9. When calculations are carried out without a digital computer, it is customary to calculate the bending moment separately for each floor of a multi-storey rigid frame, including the adjacent columns.

The third approach was to determine the ultimate strength of the structure, which had been the objective until Navier derived the elastic theory of bending in the 1820s (Section 2.3).

3.9. ULTIMATE STRENGTH DESIGN

The acceptance which the elastic theory had gained by 1930 in building codes and in textbooks on structural design obscured the fact that it was of comparatively recent origin. Load tests of structural members to destruction (Fig. 1.14) had been accepted for centuries as proof of structural safety. The test was easy to perform and it gave a definite answer. It is today still admitted in most building codes as evidence. Since the main object of structural design is to prevent failures, it is a logical method of demonstrating safety. Tests to destruction on full-scale structures are, however, far too expensive for normal design (Section 4.1). Only an ultimate strength theory, which made it unnecessary to resort constantly to testing, could compete with the elastic theory.

The relation between the stress and strain of wrought iron had been observed in the 18th century (Section 1.7). The material first deformed elastically in accordance with Hooke's Law. It then yielded, *i.e.* its deformation increased without further increase in load. This phenomenon was clearly visible in Musschenbroek's tests (Section 1.7) because the greatly increased rate of deformation at yield produced a drop in the lever arm of the testing machine. The yielding of the iron did not reduce its strength. On the contrary, there was a stiffening above the yield point, and the ultimate strength at which the iron broke was higher than its yield strength; but the yield point marked the end of the elastic deformation, and the beginning of unacceptably high *plastic deformations*. Navier (Section 2.3) had therefore based his elastic theory on the elastic range of deformation.

In 1868 H. Tresca presented two notes on plastic deformation to the French Academy of Science [68]. These were submitted to Barré de Saint-Venant, who had four years earlier edited the third edition of Navier's book. He became interested in the problem, and in 1871 wrote several papers which laid the foundations of the new subject of plasticodynamics; it is now called the theory of plasticity.

In 1914 Gabor Kazinczy in Hungary derived the plastic theory for the built-in beam (Fig. 3.10), and demonstrated that it allowed a saving in material of about 25%. The beam fails when three *plastic hinges* form (Fig. 3.10(d)), two at the supports and one at mid-span, because the statically indeterminate beam then becomes a mechanism (Section 3.3) and collapses.

In 1936 John F. Baker, Professor of Engineering at Bristol

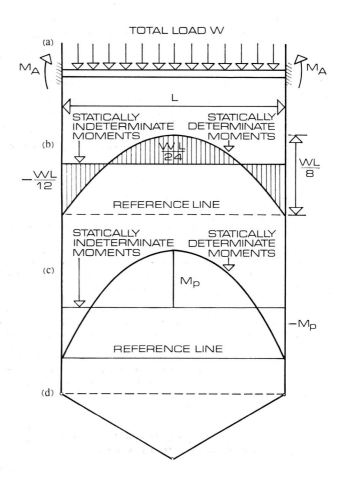

University and later Professor of Mechanical Sciences at Cambridge University, commenced a research programme to investigate the behaviour of steel structures beyond the elastic range, until sufficient plastic hinges formed to turn the structure into a mechanism so that it collapsed [112]. This problem does not have a unique solution. Even a single portal frame can collapse by the formation of plastic hinges in six different ways (Fig. 3.11). In multi-storey frames the number of possibilities is greatly increased. The critical mechanism is the one produced by the lowest load, and this may require much calculation.

In addition the frame may buckle (Section 2.5) before all the plastic hinges can form. The buckling of frames partly deformed in the plastic range is a complicated problem which has not so far been completely solved.

Single-storey rigid steel frames for industrial buildings are now frequently designed by the plastic theory; but it can be used for multi-storey buildings only if they are relatively stocky.

While the plastic theory has not been adopted in its entirety for structural design, some aspects of elastic design have been modified

---

Fig. 3.10.   Bending moments in a built-in beam according to the plastic theory. (a) The load, the span and the end-restraining moments are the same as for the elastic analysis described in Fig. 3.6. (b) Variation of bending moment according to the elastic theory (*see* Fig. 3.6(b)). (c) As the load is increased beyond the elastic range, plastic deformation begins at the points of highest bending moment, *i.e.* at the supports. This process continues until the entire steel section at the supports has turned plastic. It then forms a *hinge* which allows continued rotation without further increase in moment, *i.e.* at the constant moment M_p (the resistance moment of the fully plastic section). These two hinges counteract the two statically indeterminate moments M_A. (d) A third hinge is needed to turn the beam into a mechanism. This forms at the section of the next highest bending moment which occurs at mid-span. When the bending moment at mid-span reaches M_p, the third plastic hinge forms, the beam becomes a mechanism, and it collapses. As in Fig. 3.6, the statically determinate bending moment is $\frac{1}{8}WL$, so that, from Fig. 3.10(c)

$$2M_p = \tfrac{1}{8}WL$$

which gives $M_p = \tfrac{1}{16}WL$. This is only 75% of the maximum bending moment in the elastic state, which is $\tfrac{1}{12}WL$ (Fig. 3.6). There is thus an appreciable saving of material when the plastic theory is used.

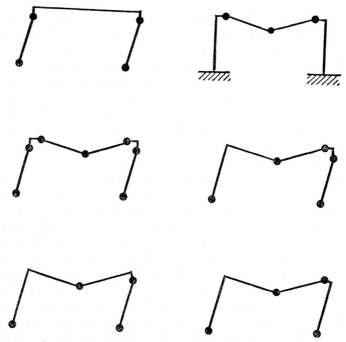

Fig. 3.11.   The six possible modes of collapse for a single portal frame built-in at the supports. The circles indicate the locations of the plastic hinges for the various collapse mechanisms.

to allow for plastic deformation, particularly in the design of steel structures.

Reinforced concrete beams also show plastic behaviour, provided the amount of reinforcement is sufficiently low to ensure that the beam fails through the gradual yielding of the reinforcement (Fig. 2.10(a)). The first ultimate strength theory was proposed in 1922 by H. Kempton Dyson, a British consulting engineer. The theory now commonly used was published in 1937 by Charles S. Whitney, an American consulting engineer [144]. This was, with some modifications, made an optional design method in the 1956 Building Code of the American Concrete Institute. In 1971 it became the standard method of design in the USA. Since then similar methods have been introduced in several European countries and in Australia.

The ultimate strength method for reinforced concrete is, however, confined to the design of the individual reinforced concrete
members. The bending moments in the rigid frame are determined
by the conventional elastic theory. This is due to the fact that the
amount of rotation possible by a reinforced concrete 'plastic' hinge
is far less than in steel. Whereas steel can be bent almost back on to
itself without breaking, reinforced concrete disintegrates after it has
been bent through a small angle. Thus the formation of the requisite
number of hinges prior to failure cannot be assumed, except for
very simple frames like that shown in Fig. 3.11.

In the 1950s the concept of *limit states design* was introduced to
unify a design procedure which was based partly on the elastic
theory, partly on the plastic theory, and partly on considerations of
durability. Thus the designer is required to satisfy simultaneously
several limit states. One limit state is the strength of the structure,
calculated partly by the elastic and partly by the plastic theory; this
gives the ultimate strength of the structure, and the actual load
which the structure can safely carry, called the working load or
service load, is obtained by dividing the ultimate load by a load
factor. Another limit state is the deflection of the structure under the
action of the service load which, if excessive, could damage brittle
finishes, cause cracks in brick or block partitions, or jam windows or
doors in the walls below. A third limit state is the deterioration of
the structure due to excessive cracking caused by insufficient
durability of the materials or to unsatisfactory design or workmanship. Limit states design has been introduced into several building
codes.

These new and more accurate methods all increase the complexity
of the design of rigid frames. Since the 1920s several methods have
been developed for mechanising the design process by the use of
mechanical models, electrical analogues and digital computers. The
last of these has been the most successful.

Chapter 4

Three-Dimensional Structures, and the Mechanisation of Structural Design

I do not like work, even if another person does it.

Mark Twain

4.1. MECHANICAL MODELS

Conceptual models have been used at least since the Renaissance. Models were built for the Duomo in Florence, for St Peter's Basilica in Rome (Section 1.5), and for many other churches. These models may have served to visualise the structure, but we know of none which were tested to determine structural sizes.

In the 19th century the elastic theory made rapid progress (Chapter 2), and empirical rules gave way to graphic statics and to structural calculations (Chapter 3). At the same time the testing of structural members became more common, and occasionally scale models of structures were tested to destruction; for example, William Fairbairn in association with Easton Hodgkinson tested in 1848 a model built to a scale of 1:7 of the tubular girders for the railway bridge over the River Conway (Section 2.5). However, during the 19th century the emphasis remained on theory.

G. E. Beggs devised his Deformeter at Princeton University in 1922 [181]. It was the first of a number of experimental methods based on an elastic theorem, derived in the 1880s by H. Müller-Breslau from Castigliano's method (Section 3.8); this had been used, particularly in Germany, for solving statically indeterminate structures. It gives a relation between the magnitude of a statically indeterminate reaction (Section 3.5), and the displacement which would occur if this reaction were removed. It is thus possible to determine the statically indeterminate reaction by means of a scale model (Fig. 4.1). Once all the statically indeterminate reactions are known, the structure becomes statically determinate, and its structural dimensions can be worked out by simple calculations.

Since the classical elastic theory is based on the assumption that deformations are small, Beggs devised equipment for producing very small deformations, and then used a micrometer microscope to measure them. This caused considerable eye strain. Larger deformations, in fact, introduce only a small error, and the first device using displacements measurable with the naked eye was the Continostat produced in 1926 by Otto Gottschalk in Germany [180].

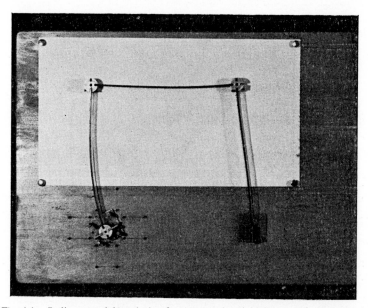

Fig. 4.1.   Indirect model analysis of a rectangular rigid frame. The horizontal, vertical and moment reactions at the left-hand support can be determined by giving it successively a horizontal displacement, a vertical displacement and a unit rotation, and measuring the deformation of the frame in each case. Once the statically indeterminate reactions are determined, the bending moment along the frame can be calculated by simple statics.

The 1920s were a decade of rapid development in the design of tall buildings, culminating in the design of the Empire State Building designed in 1927 and completed in 1931 (height 381 m or 1250 ft). Because of the Depression and World War II there was little building during the 1930s and the early 1940s, and in 1930 Hardy Cross had published the moment distribution method (Section 3.8), which provided a comparatively simple method for calculating rigid frames. Improvements in structural model testing equipment based on Beggs' Deformeter continued to be made until the 1950s [180], but these developments came too late for the design of two-dimensionally conceived frames.

The Deformeter can be used for three-dimensional design only with great difficulty, and it provides only the statically indeterminate reactions, that is, it is an indirect method of model analysis. Since the 1930s three-dimensional curved structures, as complex as any used in Gothic or Renaissance masonry (Sections 1.4 and 1.5) have been built in reinforced concrete. These structures could not be analysed by the theory of shells (Section 4.6), and their design was aided by a new, direct method of model analysis.

The first structure designed with the aid of strain measurements on a scale model was an aircraft hangar at Orvieto in Italy, designed and constructed by Pier Luigi Nervi. The structural model made to a scale of 1:30 was tested by Guido Oberti, Professor at the Milan Politecnico, in 1935. From the measured strains and deflections the stresses and deflections in the proposed structure could be deduced by dimensional theory [180]. Deflection measurements could be made easily and accurately with dial gauges, but strain measurements on structures of model size became possible only when A. U. Huggenberger, a Swiss instrument maker, developed a small lightweight mechanical gauge in the 1920s. However, these gauges could not be read by remote control, and only a few could be used on one model. During World War II the electric resistance strain gauge was developed for testing aircraft structures; this gauge is paper-thin, smaller than a postage stamp, it can be glued to the structure or model, and readings of a large number of gauges can be made from a central switchboard. These gauges were used in the late 1940s for models of shell structures (Section 4.6). Since the 1950s three-dimensional scale models (Fig. 4.2) have also been made of the skeleton frames of tall buildings (Section 4.4) to examine the three-dimensional behaviour of these structures [180 and 182].

In a model analysis the labour of computation involved in a theoretical analysis is replaced by the labour of making a suitable scale model, the necessary measurements on it, and interpreting them. There are, however, additional advantages.

Fig. 4.2. Direct structural elastic model of a 74-storey reinforced concrete building frame in Sydney, Australia, made from perspex to a scale of 1:95. The model was loaded horizontally with weights scaled to represent the maximum wind load; the resulting strains were measured with electric resistance strain gauges and the deflections with dial gauges. The structure consists of an inner tube formed by the reinforced concrete service core and an outer tube formed by the reinforced concrete columns and spandrel beams (Fig. 4.3); the two tubes are interconnected by the reinforced concrete floor slabs.

The model can be made with precisely the same restraints at the supports; in most theoretical analyses it is necessary to make some simplifying assumptions. On the other hand, model measurements are not as precise as calculations. The model thus serves as a check on the calculation, and *vice versa*.

In addition models help to clarify the structural concept. Models are thus of considerable help in making structural decisions and explaining these decisions to architects and to their clients.

4.2. ANALOGUES

There are numerous analogues for structural problems, based on various physical phenomena, notably fluid flow and electricity. Their most important application in building has been to the problem of rigid-frame design. In 1934 Vannevar Bush, the inventor of numerous successful analogues, proposed an electrical circuit in which adjustable resistors and tapped transformers were connected to simulate trusses and rigid frames of various configurations [183]. The instrument was essentially an electrical analogue for Maney's slope-deflection method (Section 3.8). The electrical components were adjusted to represent the dimensions of the structure and the loads carried by it, and the behaviour of the structure under load was then represented by electrical measurements, which took the place of calculations.

In 1953 Frederick Ryder proposed an electrical network [184] which simulated the strain-energy method (Section 3.8). Analogue computers based on this network were used commercially to solve rigid-frame problems until the 1960s, when digital computer programs were developed which performed the same task more quickly and cheaply.

4.3. CALCULATING MACHINES AND THE COMPUTER ANALYSIS OF STRUCTURES

The two main calculating aids prior to the invention of the electronic calculator were the adding machine for addition and subtraction, and the slide rule for multiplication and division. The slide rule has logarithmic scales. The sum of the logarithms of two numbers is the logarithm of their product, and addition of the numbers on a slide rule scale therefore produces multiplication.

Logarithms were invented by John Napier in 1614. Edmund Gunter plotted them on a straight line in 1620, and performed multiplication graphically with dividers. In 1633 William Oughtred used two of Gunter's lines together to perform multiplication by sliding action. In 1654 Robert Bissaker made a slide inside a fixed stock. This type of slide rule was still used in the 19th century as a common engineering aid to calculation. In 1859 Amédée Mannheim, a French artillery officer, invented the cursor, a slide with a vertical line, which greatly increased the accuracy, and he placed two square scales and a reciprocal scale on the slide rule. This type of slide rule was in general use until superseded by electronic pocket calculators in the early 1970s.

The first digital adding machine, which used rotating gear wheels, was built by Blaise Pascal in 1641. These machines also improved only slowly until the mid-19th century [185].

It was therefore common practice for engineers to use graphic statics until the later part of the 19th century in preference to methods involving arithmetic calculations (Section 3.2). When modern slide rules became available, design methods based on calculation gradually became more popular. Slide rules proved entirely adequate for the design of statically determinate and of simple statically indeterminate structures (Section 2.4, 2.7 and 3.6). It was only in the 1920s that the growing popularity of rigid-frame design created a need for mechanising structural calculations (Section 4.1), and this need became acute in the 1950s when the construction of tall buildings resumed after World War II.

It is doubtful whether electronic digital calculating machines would have been built during the same decade without the boost which World War II gave to scientific research. After the War they were applied to a variety of scientific and business problems, and in 1953 R. K. Livesley, a lecturer in engineering at the University of Manchester, published the first paper on the use of electronic digital computers for structural analysis [186]. The first commercial application reported by Livesley was to the rectangular 5-bay frame of a British power station in 1953, but it is possible that there were earlier

American applications which have not been published. At that time the structural analysis could have been done faster by conventional methods. By 1960 computerised structural analysis was cheaper for tall frames and competitive for frames of medium height; but many consulting engineers lacked satisfactory access to computers. By 1970 computerised structural analysis was in general use in America, Western Europe and Australia for all the larger frames. While model analysis and analogue computers have influenced structural analysis only marginally, digital computers have transformed it [187].

Computer-based analysis gave to statically indeterminate structures an advantage previously confined to statically determinate structures. For a statically determinate frame the forces and moments acting on the structural members can be obtained without first assuming the size of the members. Hence the sizes of the members, which are optimal for strength, can be obtained without difficulty and it is relatively simple to compare alternative designs of the structure in timber, steel and reinforced concrete. For a statically indeterminate frame it is necessary to assume the sizes of the members and the elasticity of the material in order to determine their stiffness. Optimising is therefore a very laborious process without computers. However, when a computer is used the same program can be re-run with different structural sizes and with different structural materials to obtain members which are as close to the upper limits as is permissible.

In the 1960s computer programs based on the method of finite differences were developed for the calculation of shells, and these could be used for the calculation of many curved structures for which there had previously been no analytical solution (Section 4.1).

4.4. THREE-DIMENSIONAL BUILDING FRAMES

In reality all building frames are three-dimensional. However, the earliest iron skeleton frames were conceived as an assembly of one-dimensional beams and one-dimensional columns (Section 2.4). When buildings became taller, the plane-frame concept was adopted, and this was still used in 1929 for the Empire State Building (Section

2.4), which is only slightly less in height than the Sears Tower (Fig. 4.4).

When the construction of very tall buildings resumed in the 1960s, this simple two-dimensional concept was replaced by the more economical method of designing the frame as a three-dimensional tube. Thus the columns and the spandrel beams may be considered as the horizontal and vertical members of an outer tube formed by the facade of the building (Figs. 4.2 and 4.3). Inside this outer tube is an inner tube of reinforced concrete walls which encloses the service core, required in every tall building to house the lifts and the vertical ducts for air conditioning, plumbing and electrical services.

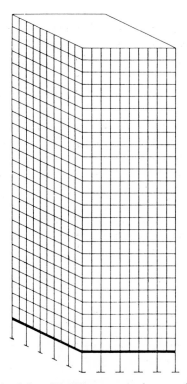

Fig. 4.3.   The facade of the tall building conceived as a perforated tube, formed by the vertical columns and the horizontal spandrel beams, with spaces between for windows.

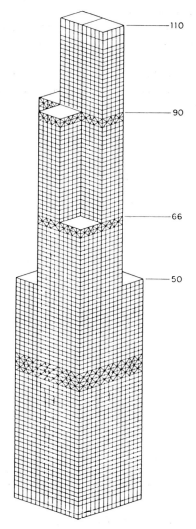

Fig. 4.4. The Sears Tower in Chicago, completed in 1974, is a 'bundle' of perforated tubes. Two of the tubes terminate at the 50th storey, two at the 66th storey, three at the 90th storey and two go the full height of 110 storeys. The diagonals are extra stiffeners surrounding the service storeys containing machinery for the lifts, air conditioning and water supply.

This concept of the tube within a tube was used by Leslie Robinson in the design of the World Trade Center, completed in New York in 1973. Its height (415 m or 1362 ft) was the first to top the Empire State Building.

In the Sears Tower (Fig. 4.4), the tallest building (442 m or 1450 ft) at the time of writing (1975), Fazlur Khan used individual tubes discontinued at different levels.

Fig. 4.5.   The 99-storey John Hancock Center in Chicago (completed in 1968) is a tube-in-tube structure with the outer tube stiffened by six sets of giant diagonals, which provide the shear resistance.

In the John Hancock Center (Fig. 4.5), the first of the tube-in-tube designs, completed in Chicago in 1968, Khan employed six sets of diagonal bracing, which give the outer tube shear resistance in the same way as diagonals do in simple trusses (Section 3.2). The giant diagonals form, however, a striking visual feature which does not please everybody.

The tube concept has been employed in many of the recently designed taller buildings, both for steel frames and for reinforced concrete frames. Since the 1960s reinforced concrete has increasingly challenged the dominance of steel as the most suitable material for tall building frames. By 1970 it had become the cheaper material for this purpose in most countries. At the time of writing (1975) the tallest buildings are steel-framed only in Canada, Japan and the USA. However, the building with the tallest reinforced concrete frame (the Water Tower Place in Chicago, which has a height of 262 m or 860 ft) is still much lower than that with the tallest steel frame.

4.5. The Return to Three-Dimensional Roof Structures

We noted in Section 2.2 that the use of iron as a principal structural material resulted in the early 19th century in a return to the simplest form of structure, namely beams supported on columns. Throughout the 19th century most engineered structures were statically determinate and most were formed by an assembly of straight members.

Buildings using traditional materials in a traditional way continued to be built side by side with these new engineered structures. In most large cities the traditionally constructed masonry buildings erected during the 19th and 20th century greatly outnumber those of earlier centuries, and more Gothic-style churches were probably built in modern times than those which survive from the entire Middle Ages.

The great structural economy, which can be achieved by the use of curvature, has been appreciated since the days of Ancient Rome. It still applies when modern materials are used, because it is ultimately necessary to provide within the structure a resistance moment equal to the moment of the applied loads (Fig. 4.6). This requires either curvature of the structural form, or thickness within the horizontal structural members, the latter being necessarily associated with heavy weights over large spans.

Some curved roof structures were built in iron and steel during the 19th century. Notable among these were the Crystal Palace

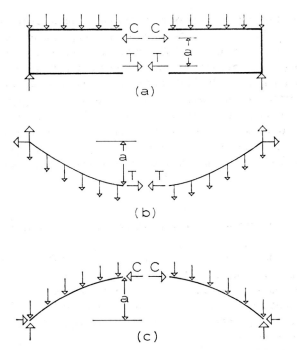

Fig. 4.6.   The vertical loads and vertical reactions impose a bending moment on the structure (Fig. 2.4) which is resisted by an internal resistance moment. (a) Resistance moment formed by the horizontal compressive force *C*, the horizontal tensile force *T* and the lever arm *within the depth* of beam *a*. The greater *a*, the greater the weight of the beam. (b) Resistance moment formed by the cable tension *T*, the horizontal reactions at the supports, and the sag of the cable *a*. An increase in *a* does not greatly add to the weight of the cable. (c) Resistance moment formed by compressive force *C* in an arch, the horizontal reactions, and the rise of the arch *a*. An increase in *a* does not greatly add to the weight of the arch.

(Section 6.6) erected for the London International Exhibition of 1851, and the arched roofs used to cover most of the main railway stations; St Pancras Station in London, designed by W. H. Barlow in 1866, still has the largest span (74 m or 243 ft) of any European railway station. For 1700 years after the construction of the Pantheon (Section 1.2) no building was erected with a longer span, but new records were now set every few years. By 1889, in the Galerie des Machines (Section 2.2), the maximum span had reached more than

$2\frac{1}{2}$ times that of the Pantheon. All these were, however, buildings for temporary exhibitions or for railways, in which people tended to wear outdoor clothing.

The use of curved iron roofs for 'indoor' buildings was more limited. Two important libraries were built with curved iron members, namely the Reading Room of the British Museum (designed by Sydney Smirke and completed in 1857) and the Bibliothèque Nationale in Paris (designed by Henri Labrouste and completed in 1868). Among other important iron structures of the 19th century are the domes of St Isaac Cathedral in St Petersburg (now Leningrad), of the Capitol in Washington, DC, and of the Royal Albert Hall in London. The last of these is the biggest dome built prior to the 20th century which is still standing; it is an oval with axes of 67 m (220 ft) and 56 m (184 ft). Iron, however, provided only the skeleton for these curved roofs and the cladding was generally of a different material. By contrast, in most traditional masonry domes and vaults, the actual roof was part of the structure.

The first reinforced concrete domes were also of ribbed construction, following the example of the earlier iron domes. In 1897 M. A. de Baudot, architect to the diocese of Paris, built a dome with reinforced concrete ribs and brick shells for the Church of Jean de Montmartre. At least six small domes entirely of reinforced concrete were built between 1900 and 1910; all had ribs.

Thereafter spans increased. The domes of the Wesleyan Hall in London (1910), of the Reading Room of the Public Library in Melbourne, Australia (1911) and of the Centenary Hall in Breslau, Germany, now Wroclaw, Poland (1913) each set a new record for span in reinforced concrete; but only the last surpassed the diameter of the Pantheon, a plain concrete dome completed in the year AD 123 (Section 1.2); in iron the Pantheon's span had already been exceeded half a century earlier.

4.6. SHELLS AND FOLDED PLATES

The reinforced concrete domes of the early 20th century were lighter than traditional masonry domes (Section 1.5), but a really thin shell cannot be produced if there are substantial flexural stresses, since the shell has to be thick enough to accommodate the lever arm (Fig. 4.6(a)).

A thin shell can exist without bending. This is easily demonstrated with a soap film, which is quite stable under tensile, compressive and shear forces acting in the surface of the membrane, but breaks immediately if subjected to bending. Thin shells are statically determinate if they are not restrained at their supports, just as triangulated trusses are statically determinate if they are pin-jointed (Section 3.2). Bending moments are induced when freedom of deformation is inhibited and the truss is then made statically indeterminate. This also applies to shells. In practice few shells can be supported to give perfectly statically determinate edge conditions, but for many the bending stresses can be restricted to a thicker edge, where the shell is supported (Fig. 4.9).

The hemispherical dome over the Planetarium in Jena (East Germany), built by the construction company Dyckerhoff and Widmann in 1923, is only 60 mm (2¾ in) thick over a span of 25 m (82 ft), and it has no ribs. The company's chief engineer, Franz Dischinger, developed the simplified membrane theory of shells for the design of this dome and later extended it to the other domes and cylindrical shells [154]. In 1936 F. Aimond added the membrane theory for the hyperbolic paraboloid [155].

Dischinger obtained the membrane solution by equating the forces in the three mutually perpendicular directions and taking moments, as in any three-dimensional statically determinate problem. Although the resulting equations look more complex than for a statically determinate frame, this is due purely to the geometry of the shell. The loads set up internal forces within the surface of the shell, i.e. direct forces in two mutually perpendicular directions and shear forces within the surface of the membrane. In a hemispherical shell, like the Jena Planetarium, there are only vertical meridional forces and horizontal hoop forces (Fig. 1.2); the shear forces in these directions are zero. The meridional forces are entirely compressive. The hoop forces are compressive in the upper portion of the dome and tensile in a broad band near the base. The meridional forces act like arches intersecting at the crown and their horizontal reaction is restrained by the tensile hoop forces near the base. The dome is therefore self-balancing. Since the hoop forces are tensile near the base of the dome, the dome expands as it is loaded; however, if the dome is supported on sufficiently flexible columns, or can slide slightly across the supporting walls, this movement can be absorbed without causing restraining moments.

In a shallow dome the meridional membrane forces require inclined reactions (Fig. 1.3(b)). In Byzantine domes (Section 1.3) this was absorbed by buttresses or semidomes acting as buttresses; this has been done in some modern shell structures, for example in the Palazetto dello Sport, built by P. L. Nervi in 1957 for the Rome Olympic Games. The simpler solution, however, is to use a circular tie to absorb these horizontal thrusts. This tie expands as the load is applied because it is in tension. However, the hoop forces in a shallow shell are entirely compressive (Fig. 1.2) and the shell itself contracts (Fig. 4.7). Consequently the tie induces bending stresses in the shell;

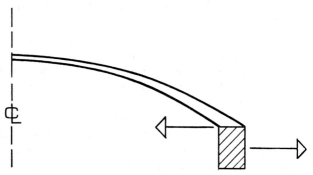

Fig. 4.7.   When a circular dome is less than hemispherical, the forces along the meridians are inclined at the supports. A ring tie is normally used to absorb the horizontal component of the meridional forces, which consequently extend under load. However, the hoop forces in a shallow dome are compressive (Fig. 1.2), so that the dome contracts under load. This incompatibility of the deformation of the edge of the shell and of the tie produces bending in the shell.

these stresses cannot be determined by statics, and they are therefore statically indeterminate.

The statically indeterminate bending theory of shells is very complicated, although for many problems exact or approximate solutions have been obtained [155 and 156]; for some simple problems, for example small domes, empirical rules suffice for thickening the shell near its junction with the tie and for adding reinforcement to resist the bending moment.

In the late 1960s computer programs were developed to produce numerical results for shells for which there are no general solutions; these are mostly based on the method of finite elements (Section 4.3). However, at that time the popularity of shell structures was already on the wane.

The reason for the extensive use of shells in the late 1940s and the early 1950s in Europe and America was partly due to the steel shortage following World War II, which limited the use of steel trusses for industrial buildings, such as single-storey factories and garages. The damage done to uncased steel structures through fire started by aerial bombardment may have been a contributing factor. In the 1960s rising labour costs made curved concrete structures less attractive in Western Europe and North America, although their popularity continued in Eastern Europe, South America and India.

The reinforced concrete shells of the 1920s and 1930s had continued the tradition of masonry construction. They covered great interior spaces with domes and cylindrical vaults, although these were much lighter than traditional masonry structures. These buildings were, however, relatively few in number.

The majority of the shell structures built after World War II were multiple roofs for utilitarian structures, which presumed regular column spacing. A few domes were built on rectangular plans, but cylindrical shells were better suited for this purpose.

There are basically two types of cylindrical shell. One is called the *short shell* because the straight lines run in the short direction; the other is called a *long shell*, because the straight lines run in the long direction (Fig. 4.8). Both require transverse ties or end frames to prevent the curved slab from flattening out. In the short shell the arch action predominates, so that this shell can be designed by the membrane theory with some correction for the bending induced by the ties or end frames. In long shells the arch action is subordinate to the bending action, and the membrane theory cannot be used for these shells. However, a good approximation to the precise bending theory of shells is obtained by considering the shells to act like a straight beam of curved cross section (Fig. 4.8).

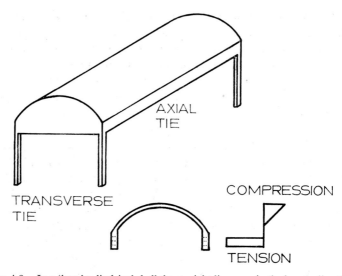

Fig. 4.8.   In a 'long' cylindrical shell the straight lines run in the longer direction. Transverse ties are essential to prevent the shell from spreading. Axial ties help to accommodate the main reinforcement, but they are not essential. The shell can, as a first approximation, be considered as a curved beam. The concrete at the crown resists the flexural compression and the reinforcement in the axial ties resists the flexural tension.

The membrane stresses in domes and cylindrical shells are comparatively small, particularly near the crown, and thus large openings can be cut to admit natural light, if desired. Reinforcement is only nominal over the greater part of the surface, except where the shell is supported directly on the columns, which causes high stress concentrations requiring heavy reinforcement. Both these aspects are shown in Fig. 4.9, which illustrates one of the first shallow thin concrete domes to be built without ribs and with a large skylight. The longest spanning building erected so far (1975) is the Palais du Centre National des Industries et des Techniques (CNIT Exhibition Hall) in Paris, completed in 1958. It is a double shell with a span of 219 m (719 ft), each shell having a thickness of 60 mm ($2\frac{3}{8}$ in), separated by a space of 3·75 m (12 ft 4 in), with stiffening diaphragms at 9 m (30 ft) centres. This is a return to Brunelleschi's concept of the double dome of Florence Cathedral (Section 1.5).

The revival of traditional masonry forms, namely domes and cylindrical shells, was a natural first step in the design of reinforced concrete shells. In masonry structures the cost of cutting blocks is not greatly affected by the geometry of the structure, once one gets away from rectangular blocks, and domes were relatively easy to build because each ring of masonry blocks was stable under its own weight, until the angle of inclination of the joints became too great

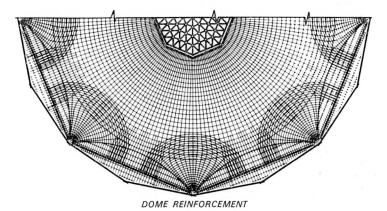

DOME REINFORCEMENT

Fig. 4.9.   Arrangement of the reinforcement in the Market Hall at Algeciras, Spain, designed by Eduardo Torroja in 1933 and destroyed during the Spanish Civil War. The polygonal dome spanned 47·5 m (156 ft), and the thickness of the concrete shell was 90 mm ($3\frac{1}{2}$ in), increasing gradually to 450 mm (18 in) at the columns to withstand the bending stresses caused by the 'point' supports. The reinforcement closely followed the stress trajectories, which are the lines of maximum tension.

for friction to hold the blocks in position. The economics of concrete structures is, however, largely determined by the cost of the form-work.

Because it is impossible to generate a dome with straight lines, there is no simple way of building the timber formwork of a concrete dome without cutting the timber at an angle. The additional cost of the formwork has made domes less attractive for small spans. For large spans the linearity of the timber is less important because the radius of curvature is much larger than the length of the timber.

There are only two surfaces on which two series of straight lines can be drawn. One is the hyperboloid formed by a straight line rotating about an axis, and familiar from its use for cooling towers. Its geometry was first described in 1669 by Christopher Wren, at that time Professor of Astronomy at Oxford University, before he acquired fame as an architect.

The other is the hyperbolic paraboloid, generated by a straight line moving over two other straight lines at an angle to one another. It was discovered in the late 19th century and in the 1930s F. Aimond, an engineer with the French Railways, worked out its membrane theory and designed several engine sheds roofed with hyperbolic paraboloids. In the 1950s Felix Candela demonstrated its architectural versatility in a number of roof structures, noteworthy both for their low cost and their elegance. Most of these shells had small spans. Since then hyperbolic paraboloid shells with larger spans have been constructed, notably in the USA (Fig. 4.10).

Fig. 4.10.   Roof for a convention centre in Colorado Springs, Colorado, formed by four hyperbolic paraboloids arranged with a common horizontal centre ridge. The outside edges have ribs which rest at their lowest points on steel tripods held by concrete abutments; these are tied together with prestressing cables (Section 3.4). The span is 54·8 m (180 ft), the shell thickness is 75 mm (3 in) and the reinforcement is placed parallel to the diagonals of the shell. (Architects: Francis and Guy; Structural Engineers: Ketchum, Konkel and Hastings.)

The folded plate structure, composed of flat plates connected at various angles, provides another approach to the linearisation of shells. When the curvature is eliminated, bending stresses must result (Fig. 4.6), and folded plates are subject to some bending. However, the cost of the formwork for flat surfaces is less than that of any shell, including a shell generated by straight lines. For spans of about 20 m (66 ft) the thickness of the concrete structure is determined less by the stresses in it than by constructional limitations, such as the minimum depth which a contractor is able to cast with the requisite dimensional accuracy and the need for a waterproof roof. A concrete slab 80 mm ($3\frac{1}{4}$ in) thick is capable of resisting some bending and this is frequently sufficient for the bending moments in folded plates of moderate span.

Folded plates fulfil functions similar to domes and vaults and have comparable, if different, aesthetic qualities. They were first used in Germany in the 1920s for coal bunkers without supporting beams, their design being based on the slope-deflection method (Section 3.8). In 1947 George Winter, Professor of Structural Engineering at Cornell University, developed a much simpler moment distribution method [157]. In the 1950s the development of waterproof plywood and of hardboard (Section 6.5) made available easily cut sheet material suitable for concrete formwork at a reasonable cost and folded plates became notably more economical.

4.7. Space Frames

While the folded plate structure replaces the shell by a number of flat slabs, the ribbed shell replaces it by a series of linear, if not necessarily straight elements. It varies from the fine mesh of the decorative precast concrete units employed by Pier Luigi Nervi [138], which provide the roof surface, to the coarse grid of the geodesic domes popularised by Buckminster Fuller, which merely provide the skeleton for the roof cover [160].

It is debatable whether a structure built in the shape of a shell (Fig. 4.11), but having a greater volume of voids than solid material within the surface, may be regarded as a shell structure. Its overall structural behaviour is that of a shell, but the design of the individual members is determined by the character of the structure as an inter-connected frame [161].

The simplest space frame, like the simplest plane frame, consists of an assembly of triangles and this structure can be worked out by statics alone if the members are pin-jointed, *i.e.* if the connections are not rigid. The concept is due to J. W. A. Schwedler [158] who built the first triangulated iron dome over a gas tank in Berlin in 1863

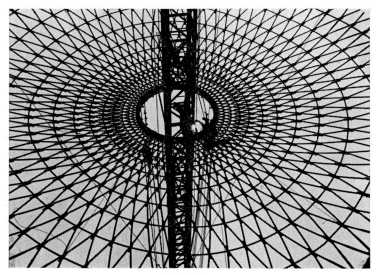

Fig. 4.11.   Erection of the dome of the Big Exhibition Pavilion, Brno, Czecho-slovakia. The triangulated structure, made from steel tubes and spanning 92 m (302 ft), was designed by F. Lederer in the late 1950s.

with a span of 30 m (98 ft). Schwedler's domes were formed by vertical ribs corresponding to the meridians of longitude on the earth's surface, horizontal members following the circles of latitude (which are 'small circles' in spherical trigonometry), and diagonals which performed the triangulation. Schwedler analysed these domes by the Method of Resolution at the Joints (Section 3.2).

Karl Culmann developed a graphic method (Section 3.2) which determined the three-dimensional stress diagram by projection on horizontal and vertical planes.

In 1920 Richard Southwell devised the Method of Tension Coefficients for the design of airship frames. He expressed the sines and cosines in the Method of Resolution at the Joints in terms of Cartesian coordinates, that is, x, y and z. The simultaneous equations are much easier to evaluate in this form, particularly if they are written in matrix algebra. However, the problem created by the laborious arithmetic of space frames was not really solved until digital computers came into use (Section 4.3).

Triangulated steel domes are well suited to roofs of sporting arenas. The two largest are the Harris County Stadium, or Astrodome, in Houston, Texas, built in the 1960s with a span of 196 m (643 ft), and the Louisiana Superdome in New Orleans, completed in 1973 with a span of 207 m (679 ft); this is, however, less than the span of the CNIT Exhibition Hall (Section 4.6). These large domes have stiff joints, they are consequently statically indeterminate (Section 3.3), and a large computer is required for their analysis.

An alternative to Schwedler's method of triangulation is to use identical spherical triangles for the entire dome surface, formed by great circles only. This method was used in the Dome of Discovery, an aluminium dome with a steel tension ring built for the 1951 London International Exhibition and later demolished. Richard Buckminster Fuller has called the great-circle dome the *geodesic dome*, and he patented it in 1954. He has designed many geodesic domes ranging from a large repair shed for railway cars at Baton Rouge, Louisiana, built in 1958 with a span of 117 m (384 ft), to small climbing frames for children [160].

Space frames have also been used for long-span flat roofs, notably for aircraft hangars and factories. Space frames generally use less material for the same column spacing than an assembly of plane frames, but jointing is expensive because triangulation in three dimensions is required [162 and 164].

4.8. SUSPENSION STRUCTURES AND PNEUMATIC STRUCTURES

Suspension cables have the greatest potential for span; the cable is in tension and bending stresses, which require additional depth, are eliminated (Fig. 4.6) by its flexibility. Arches cannot be flexible, and they must consequently have exactly the right shape to be in pure compression; moreover, they are not as efficient because of the problem of buckling (Section 2.5). Since 1826 the longest spanning bridge has always been a suspension bridge, except for an interval of 40 years when the record was held by two cantilever bridges, namely the Forth Bridge (Fig. 3.4) and the Quebec Bridge in Canada.

Single suspension cables are statically determinate (Fig. 4.6(b)). In a roof structure, however, additional cables are required at right angles to support the roof sheeting and, for stability, these cables must be interconnected to form a net. The resulting structure is statically indeterminate. A steel cable 100 m (328 ft) long expands 30 mm (1·2 in) due to a change of temperature of 2·5°C (4·5°F). It is necessary to prestress the cables in one direction to ensure that they do not become loose on a hot day and damage the roof sheeting by wind-induced flutter.

The first suspension roof was completed in 1953 for the arena at the State Fair in Raleigh, North Carolina; Maciej Novicki (who died before construction started) and Fred N. Severud were the structural designers. The structure consists of two intersecting arches hinged at their supports and at their joints. These carry the suspension cables spanning 99 m (325 ft). At right angles to these loadbearing cables are secondary cables which are prestressed. Since then a number of suspension structures have been built, hanging from intersecting arches, outer compression rings, and supporting columns or walls [163, 164 and 165]. Several have been designed like tents (Fig. 4.12).

F. W. Lanchester, the pioneer of the British automobile industry, conceived the pneumatic structure in 1917 to roof army field hospitals, but the War ended before any could be built. He explained that a roof of balloon fabric could be supported by a very small air pressure in excess of atmospheric pressure. Entry to the building would be by airlocks [104]. The first pneumatic roofs were actually built in 1946 by Walter Bird to cover the instruments of the American Early Defence Warning Line through northern Canada and Alaska. Pneumatic roof structures perform satisfactorily with an excess air pressure of only 70 mm of water pressure (685 Pa, or 14·3 psf, or $6·8 \times 10^{-3}$ atmospheres); this is an increase of 0·7% above external atmospheric pressure. This excess pressure is maintained with an air compressor, which replaces any air pressure lost through the fabric and at the revolving doors as people enter and leave [164 and 166].

These roofs have been used for a small number of assembly plants, warehouses, temporary classrooms, temporary hospital wards and also for a theatre in Boston, Massachusetts [166]. In 1970 pneumatic structures became the architectural theme of the Osaka International Exposition [164], as suspension structures had been at the Brussels International Exposition of 1958.

Fig. 4.12.   Sidney Myer Music Bowl in Melbourne, Australia, a 3700 m² (40 000 sq ft) canopy of aluminium-bonded plywood supported on flexible suspension cables. It was completed in 1957. (Architects: Yuncken, Freeman Brothers, Griffiths and Simpson; Structural Engineers: Irwin and Johnson.)

In the 1960s Dante Bini, an Italian architect, started to use air-supported membranes as the formwork for casting concrete domes (Fig. 4.13). Previous attempts to cast concrete domes on inflated membranes had been unsuccessful because it is impossible in practice to cast a big concrete dome on top of a balloon or to spray it with a concrete gun without distorting the shape due to the uneven distribution of the concrete during placement. Bini cast the concrete on the ground on top of a folded membrane and then inflated the membrane. The concrete, between 40 and 70 mm ($1\frac{1}{2}$ to $2\frac{3}{4}$ in) thick, was reinforced with springs which expanded as the balloon was inflated and which controlled the shape of the dome.

Fig. 4.13.   Concrete dome for library in Narrabeen, NSW, built in 1975, by the inflation of a membrane after the concrete had been placed. The holes for doors and windows were cut after the concrete had hardened, and an insulating layer was sprayed on both the inside and the outside of the concrete dome. (Architect: Dante Bini; Structural Engineers: Taylor, Thomson and Whitting.)

4.9. THE SOLUTION OF THE PROBLEM OF SPAN

In the middle of the 19th century the Pantheon (Section 1.2), a concrete dome built in the year AD 123, was still the building with the longest span, namely 43 m (141 ft). In the second half of the 19th century iron structures, and later steel structures, were built with rapidly increasing spans and by 1890 the longest span was $2\frac{1}{2}$ times as great. The first reinforced concrete dome to surpass the span of the Pantheon was the Centenary Hall in Wroclaw, in 1912 (Section 4.5). At present (1975) the CNIT Exhibition Hall in Paris (Section 4.6), completed in 1958, has the longest span of 219 m (719 ft), five times that of the Pantheon. There is no apparent advantage in a greater span, unless it were to roof an entire city, so that the problem of span, which has been a prime preoccupation of architects and their clients since Roman times, may be regarded as solved.

The reduction in the amount of building material required to achieve this large span, and thus a corresponding reduction in cost, is even more impressive. One cannot compare an ancient concrete or masonry structure with a steel structure, which uses more expensive material, but a comparison with a modern reinforced concrete structure is not unreasonable. The dome of the Pantheon has an average thickness of 4 m (13 ft), so that the ratio of span to thickness is 11. The combined average thickness of the masonry shells of the Duomo in Florence (Section 1.5) is 2 m (6 ft 7 in), which gives a span to thickness ratio of 21. St Paul's in London (Section 1.5), the lightest of the classical domes, has a ratio of 37. The Jena Planetarium (Section 4.6) has a ratio of 420. The combined thickness of the double shell of the CNIT Exhibition Hall is 120 mm ($4\frac{3}{4}$ in), which gives a ratio of 1800. For a pneumatic roof (Section 4.8) the ratio is of the order of 20 000, but the material is more expensive than concrete. As a matter of interest, the span to thickness ratio for a hen's egg is about 100.

Chapter 5

Environmental Design Replaces Structure as the Principal Problem of Building Science

> It is probable that all existing whispering galleries, it is certain
> that the six more famous ones, are accidents; it is equally
> certain that all could have been predetermined without
> difficulty, and like most accidents improved upon.
>
> *W. C. Sabine*

5.1. THE CONFLICT BETWEEN STRUCTURAL LIGHTNESS AND ENVIRONMENTAL EFFICIENCY

Except for a brief interlude during the late era of the Roman Republic and during the Roman Empire, environmental design received little attention prior to the 18th century. Good acoustics and sound insulation were the result of accident. The level of artificial light was low, heating was primitive and artificial cooling was impossible.

The environmental quality of many buildings surviving from the Middle Ages and the Renaissance is, nevertheless, surprisingly good. Even if artificial light was lacking, the quality of the natural lighting was often very agreeable. Music composed during the Middle Ages, the Renaissance and the Baroque generally sounds better in the buildings of the time than in a modern concert hall, because the music was composed to fit the buildings in which it was to be performed. Thick masonry walls provided sound and heat insulation.

The development of structural engineering did not alter these conditions during the 19th century. Walls continued to be built of solid masonry, and better heating improved thermal conditions during the winter. However, during the 20th century the thick walls were gradually replaced by thin curtain walls, and glass was used to an increasing extent to emphasise the lightness of the structure and to increase the floor area available for lease. All but four of the ground floor columns were often eliminated, sometimes because of the commercial value of large open spaces at ground-floor level, but sometimes merely to show that the building did not need loadbearing walls.

Many of the pioneers of modern architecture had a good knowledge of structural systems and they used the lightness of engineered structures as an important element in design. Few of them (Frank Lloyd Wright was one of the exceptions) had initially a sufficient appreciation of the environmental consequences of substituting thin walls, and particularly glass walls, for the traditional thick masonry walls. Air conditioning, introduced in the 1920s, became common in the 1950s (Section 5.4) and in the era following World War II architects tended to hand over the environmental design to mechanical–electrical consulting engineers, who introduced as much air conditioning and artificial lighting as might be necessary to achieve an acceptable interior environment. In the late 19th century (Section 1.1) there had been a similar lack of rapport between the architect and the structural engineer, which often produced unnecessarily heavy structures.

In the 1960s there was a reaction against the excessive use of electricity to correct the environmental defects of buildings. This was partly because a new generation of architects was better informed about environmental design, partly because of a general reaction against the philosophy of the affluent society, and partly because the electric power supply in some important cities, such as New York, was unable to cope with the fast increasing demand; a large part of this demand was created by the services of major city buildings.

At the same time there was a reduced interest in erecting buildings with large spans and with spectacularly light skeleton frames. Once spans of 200 m (656 ft) were reached, there was no apparent advantage to be gained from increasing spans further. The expression of structural lightness also reached its ultimate limit by the 1950s. The emphasis now shifted to the creation of the perfect interior environment, with the fabric of the building contributing as much as possible. The *avant-garde* architecture of the 1950s was intended to impress by its structure, but the mark of a good environmental design is rather that one fails to notice anything disagreeable or uncomfortable.

5.2. Climate, Thermal Comfort and the Design of Buildings

The Ancient Greeks divided the earth's surface into climatic zones according to their inclination to the equator; indeed, the original meaning of the Greek word *klima* is inclination. This concept of climatic zones assumed a motionless atmosphere. The effect of air movement on climate was first discussed in a paper by Alexander von Humboldt in 1817, in which he introduced the concept of isothermal lines to illustrate weather patterns. The first weather maps were drawn in the 1830s. Climatological data have become particularly important since the development of air conditioning, because they provide the basis for calculating the capacity of the plant required.

Although climatology is thus a modern science, there are empirical rules dating back to ancient times. Vitruvius [11] recommended that bedrooms should face east, a precept still widely followed today. Some ancient rules are, however, based on superstition. Vitruvius counselled against natural ventilation because 'cold winds are disagreeable, hot winds are enervating and moist winds unhealthy'. This reluctance to admit fresh air continued through the Middle Ages.

Until the end of the 19th century it was widely believed that the discomfort which resulted from the presence of a large number of people in a room was due to toxic gases produced by the people. A. L. Lavoisier, who discovered the composition of the atmosphere, thought that this substance was carbon dioxide, and various compounds exhaled from the skin and from the lungs had been considered.

In 1905 J. S. Haldane established that temperature, humidity and air movement were the criteria for human comfort and, in 1914, Leonard Hill disproved the theory that a toxic substance was responsible. He shut a group of people in a room, then through a window observed their increasing distress as temperature, humidity and carbon dioxide content increased. Turning on a fan provided great relief. Another group made to breathe the same air at normal temperature suffered no distress [220]. In the course of this investigation Hill developed the *katathermometer* for measuring the effect of air movement on the human body. It was a thermometer with a large bulb heated to a little above body temperature, and allowed to cool by the air current through 5°F (2·8°C), which indicated the effect of air movement on the human body.

Several additional instruments have been devised to predict the reaction of people to thermal comfort under various conditions. The most elaborate was A. F. Dufton's eupatheoscope [225], which consisted of an electrically heated cylinder with a thermostat inside. When the thermostat reached 25·5°C, the heating current was switched off until its temperature dropped below 25·5°C. As the instrument took account of temperature, air movement and radiation, it was thus particularly suited to standardising comfort conditions in a cool climate. The temperature of an environment which required the same power input Dufton called the *equivalent temperature*.

Although physical measurements give objective answers, the alternative approach of interviewing a group of observers has been more successful. In the investigation by F. C. Houghten and C. P. Yaglou in Pittsburgh, Pa., in 1922 [224] a group of people were asked what conditions of temperature, humidity and air movement gave the same sensation of thermal comfort or discomfort while they were engaged in light physical work; this was called the *effective temperature*. Since it takes account of the effect of air movement, but ignores radiation, this criterion is particularly well suited to warm-weather conditions.

Effective temperature was included in the Handbook of the American Society of Heating and Ventilating Engineers (now ASHRAE, the American Society of Heating, Refrigeration and Air Conditioning Engineers) as the criterion of design for thermal comfort until the late 1950s. It was then replaced by a series of 43 charts devised by P. O. Fanger [226], Professor at the Danmarks Tekniske Højskole, who worked at one time at the ASHRAE research laboratories. These charts take account also of radiation and of the amount of clothing worn.

The thermal comfort criteria required some modification for the tropics. The voyages of discovery, which started at the same time as the European Renaissance (Section 1.5), had led to the colonisation of Africa, Asia and America. It was widely believed that the native people of the tropics were the only ones who could work satisfactorily in a hot climate, but in the 20th century it was recognised that acclimatisation is in fact a deliberate lowering of efficiency to that appropriate to the climate [222]. It followed that human efficiency in the tropics could be increased by improvements in the indoor climate. In countries inhabited by people with a sufficiently high income, such as the southern USA or northern Australia, air conditioning provided an answer, but in the newly independent ex-colonies the lower incomes made this impracticable. Traditional solutions were studied [223] and some were found to be applicable to developed as well as developing countries.

Many native buildings in the hot–humid tropics were built from timber slats, bamboo or reeds which allowed the free passage of natural ventilation, and thus reduced the effective temperature [224]. In the hot–arid tropics thick walls built from mud, mudbrick or masonry reduced the indoor temperature at the hottest time of the day. At night the interior remained hotter than the air outside the buildings, but people traditionally slept in the open air during the hot weather. Many architects have thus looked to vernacular construction as an inspiration. However, this has led to some mistakes, since traditional solutions are not always climatologically correct.

5.3. Sun Control

Sun shades have been used in many parts of the world. In Muslim architecture roof overhangs shading the windows were a common feature, particularly in Iran and in India. In hot–arid climates a pool of water was often added; its evaporation lowered the temperature and increased the humidity. The verandah developed in India and it was introduced into several British colonies, including Australia (Fig. 5.1). In the southern USA, the Greek Revival style achieved great popularity during the 19th century, at least partly because the roof overhang supported on columns provided sunshading.

Summer is hot in most parts of North America and roof overhangs have been used by many American architects. Most of the 'prairie' houses built by Frank Lloyd Wright in and around Chicago between 1889 and 1910 had carefully designed roof overhangs.

However, roof overhangs were disliked by many architects of the Modern Movement.

In 1933 Le Corbusier built the Cité de Refuge, a hostel for the Salvation Army in Paris, with the object of giving its 600 inhabitants 'the full light of the sun'. The building was agreeably warm during the winter, but much too hot in the summer, and the southern facade was subsequently fitted with sunshades. For the Ministry of Education in Rio de Janeiro, completed in 1937, Le Corbusier consequently

Fig. 5.1.   Verandah in a 19th-century house in Sydney, Australia, with cast iron columns and railings.

advised the use of adjustable sunshades built integrally with the building (*brise soleil*), and these were particularly popular in the late 1940s and early 1950s. The various angles at which adjustable *brise soleil* can be set give, however, a disorderly appearance to the facade, and moreover it is difficult to maintain their adjustability, *i.e.* they have a tendency to become stuck in one position. Fixed sunshades are more practical and single shades over the windows offer the least obstruction to natural lighting and ventilation, and to the view from the windows [219].

The information required to calculate the roof overhang was already known in the 2nd century AD; it is given in Book III of Ptolemy's *Almagest*. However, it is likely that roof overhangs prior to the 20th century were determined empirically, or by considering the utilisation of the space under the overhang. Thus the width of the Indian and Australian verandah (Fig. 5.1) was usually greater than that required for sunshading, and the interior of the houses was consequently unnecessarily dark.

In 1932 A. F. Dufton devised the heliodon [218] for determining experimentally the sunshading required and several sun-machines have been developed since then (Fig. 5.2).

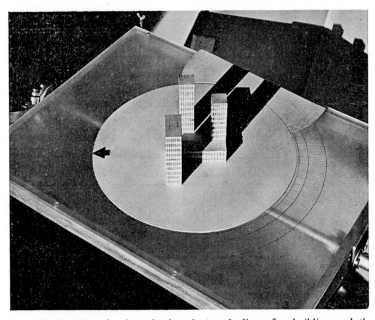

Fig. 5.2. Heliodon for investigating the sunshading of a building and the penetration of sunlight into its interior. The sun is modelled by a horizontal spotlight placed as far as practicable from the rotating table. The altitude is adjusted by rotating the table through a worm gear. The azimuth is adjusted by rotating the model on the table which has a graduated circular scale. Interior observations can be made through the transparent table top. The altitude and the azimuth are calculated from the orientation of the building relative to the north point, from its latitude, from the day of the year and from the time of the day. In another type of heliodon the light representing the sun is mounted at the end of an arm and rotated by two screws graduated respectively for the day of the year and for the time of the day. The table is adjusted according to the latitude of the building. Because the lamp is much nearer to the model the result is less accurate, but it is not necessary to calculate the altitude and the azimuth of the sun.

In colder climates the opposite problem arises. Tall buildings can obstruct the sunlight necessary for adequate daylighting. G. Pleijel developed the globoscope for the study of this problem in Sweden in the late 1940s. It consists of a paraboloidal mirror, in which a distorted image of the surrounding buildings is seen in stereographic projection, as observed from above. The sunlight penetration can be studied by superimposing a transparent sun-path diagram.

The equations for the movement of the sun are expressed in terms of spherical trigonometry with the data for the position of the sun varying with the latitude, the time of the day, and the time of the year. The calculations were somewhat laborious by slide rule and the sun-machines were developed for this reason.

The digital computer (Section 4.3) has been used in the 1970s for the graphical solution of sunlight penetration. A graphic output unit draws the sunlight penetration in plan and in four elevations. The paper can then be folded to form a three-dimensional model.

5.4. Heating, Ventilation and Air Conditioning

Improvement of a cold environment by heating is as old as the use of fire by primitive man. Fixed fireplaces have been found in houses in Troy, dating from about 2000 BC, and in other contemporary settlements. An open fire was lit in the centre of the room and the smoke escaped through a hole in the roof. This method was still used in some of the royal palaces of England in the 15th century AD. Because this simple method does not work in multi-storey buildings, flues and chimneys were first used in the keeps of castles in the 13th century. Grates were introduced in England in the 16th century; previously the fuel had been placed in a heap on the floor.

The Greeks and the Romans used charcoal braziers for heating and these were often elaborately decorated objects of bronze. In the colder climates of Germany and The Netherlands large braziers became in the 16th century fully enclosed metal stoves [227]. Reports of tile stoves also go back to the 16th century (Fig. 5.3). In Eastern Europe large ceramic stoves became a part of the interior decoration. In palaces they were often moulded by famous sculptors and the refuelling was done from a special passage built for the purpose.

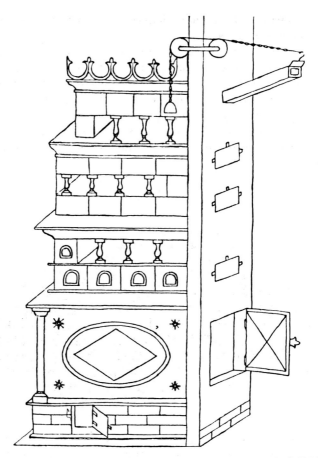

Fig. 5.3.   Swedish tile stove from the 17th century. (From Ref. 227.)

The most advanced heating system prior to the 19th century was the Roman hypocaust, which originated in the 1st century BC, and was described in detail by Vitruvius [11].

It was at first used for the hot rooms in the public baths, but subsequently also in the villas of wealthy citizens in the colder parts of the Roman Empire. The ruins of numerous hypocausts can be seen from Turkey to Spain and from Africa to Britain; in England there are substantial remains at Bath (Aquae Sulis) and at St Albans (Verulamium) (Fig. 5.4).

The hypocaust was formed by passages under the floor. Hot gases from a furnace at one end passed to a chimney at the other end; these heated the floor surface. These passages were about 150 mm (6 in) wide, and formed by brick piers, about 450 mm (18 in) square by 600 mm (24 in) high. On top of these piers were placed *bipedales*, thin Roman bricks two Roman feet ($23\frac{1}{4}$ in or 579 mm) square. The floor on top of these bricks was generally of concrete paved with mosaic.

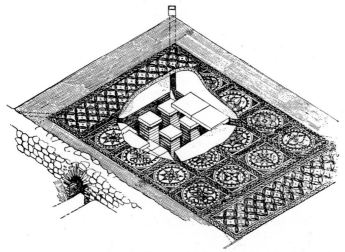

Fig. 5.4.   Hypocaust heating beneath a mosaic floor in St Albans (the Roman Verulamium). The furnace entrance is on the left and the chimney on the right. The smoke passed between the brick pillars to heat the floor. (From Ref. 189.)

Modern methods of heating date from the Industrial Revolution. The earliest British factories were unheated, as most factories in China (whose northern cities have very cold weather in winter) are to this day. In 1784 James Watt, the inventor of the condensing steam engine, used waste steam from his plant to heat his own office, and later the entire factory. In the first decade of the 19th century both Watt and William Strutt (Section 2.2) used waste steam for heating factories.

In 1792 Strutt used gravity warm-air heating for the new hospital in Derby, paid for by subscriptions from local industrialists. The Derbyshire General Infirmary was the first of a number of properly heated hospitals, and thereafter hospitals, many financed by industrialists, became leaders in the art of heating. Joseph Bramah, better known as the inventor of the Bramah hydraulic press, installed hot-water radiators to heat Westminster Hospital shortly afterwards.

In Britain the open fireplace was preferred until the middle of the 20th century, and prior to 1914 there were plenty of servants to tend these fires in the houses of the upper and the middle classes.

In North America, where the climate was more severe, and where servants were scarce and expensive, the technology of heating overtook that of Britain during the 19th century.

Even domestic heating was usually generated by boilers which in time became more and more automatic. The actual heating units were cast-iron hot-water or steam radiators. Towards the end of the 19th century some of the wealthier American houses were both heated and ventilated by hot air, supplied to the rooms through plenum ducts, *i.e.* ducts operating under a slight excess of pressure. Because of this excess pressure there were no draughts. By comparison the British open fires produced a big flow of air up the chimney, which had to be balanced by an air intake under the door and through any badly fitting windows. These created the draughts for which many of England's stately homes were famous.

Hospitals were also leaders of progress in ventilation. This was at least partly due to the widely held theory that the malaise resulting from crowded rooms was produced by toxic gases produced by the people (Section 5.2). The Derbyshire General Infirmary, built in 1792 and mentioned above, had a system of mechanical ventilation. In America ventilation by plenum ducts was common for hospitals by the 1870s [228]. In 1895 a wet air-screen was installed in the Victoria Hospital in Glasgow whereby dust and soot particles were removed by washing.

In 1906 Stuart W. Cramer in Charlotte, North Carolina, used individual heads spraying chilled water to clean and cool the air. He called this method *air conditioning*. The more effective method, however, was devised in the same year by Willis H. Carrier [230], whereby the moisture content was controlled by chilling the air. As the temperature was reduced, the dew point was reached at which the air became saturated with water vapour and the excess was condensed. When the desired moisture content had been achieved by cooling, the air was re-heated to the desired temperature.

In 1922 Carrier used this system for the first fully air-conditioned building, Graumann's Metropolitan Theater in Los Angeles. The air was cooled by a refrigeration plant to the temperature whose dew point corresponded to the required humidity. It was then heated to the required temperature, fed into the auditorium through diffusers in the ceiling, and exhausted through grilles under the seats.

The number of air-conditioned buildings was relatively small until the late 1940s. However, the wartime technological advances transformed air conditioning from a luxury to a civilised amenity. Most of the important American buildings erected since that time have been air-conditioned. Other industrialised countries followed a decade later. The technical perfection of the interior thermal environment by air conditioning [229] arrived just in time for the era of the curtain wall (Section 5.1).

The extraordinarily fast rate at which air conditioning was being produced, particularly in the USA, created a demand for electricity, which by the early 1970s power stations in some cities, for example New York, had difficulty in meeting. The sudden increase in the price of oil in 1973 also drew attention to the predictions of an eventual exhaustion of traditional energy sources, which had been made for several decades, but ignored the potentialities of solar energy. Solar water heaters had been used for many years [231], but in most countries the saving in fuel did not compensate for the extra capital cost until the great increase in the price of oil.

5.5. NATURAL AND ARTIFICIAL LIGHTING

Prior to the 19th century natural lighting was the main source of illumination. Since at least 2500 BC artificial lighting had been provided by oil lamps, many of which have been found in archaeological excavations; these probably used vegetable or fish oil. It is likely that candles made from tallow and beeswax were also used from an early age. However, with the exception of beeswax which was not available in large quantities, the raw materials for lighting were also edible; thus in times of food shortage there was a tendency to economise on light [232].

The size of windows is not purely determined by the amount of daylight required. During the Middle Ages, when security was a problem even within the city walls, windows tended to be small and narrow, except in churches which were regarded as sanctuaries. During the Gothic era church windows increased greatly in size, at least partly because the forces were carried by the buttresses (Section 1.4) rather than by loadbearing walls, so that larger openings could be made for glass. Most of the Gothic churches were built in the temperate zone, where large windows have always been welcome.

The windows in the palazzi of the Italian Renaissance were notably smaller to limit the admission of undesirable heat; but, when the Renaissance was adopted in England, the windows in the classical facades tended to become much larger (Fig. 5.5).

Interior courts had been built into medieval and Renaissance palaces, partly for security reasons, and partly to admit additional daylight. During the 19th century, as the newfound industrial and commercial activities greatly increased the demand for light, these interior courts multiplied in number. They were often reduced to the bare minimum necessary to admit light. Sometimes they were given a glass roof to admit light but to keep out rain, and eventually they became open spaces in a building under a glass roof. These lightwells disappeared only with the improvement of electric lighting.

In the 18th century the new sperm whale fisheries supplemented the supplies of wax and tallow. Candle-making became mechanised and, in the houses of the wealthy, vast chandeliers with numerous candles came into use.

In the 19th century petroleum became available for lighting. Mineral oil had been used since antiquity. Pliny described a mineral oil which could be used directly in lamps. Most natural petroleum was, however, too thick for this purpose and the oil which was found from time to time in the Middle East and in America generally had no practical use. In 1847 E. W. Binney, a Manchester chemist, distilled petroleum found in Derbyshire and produced lamp oil. Within a few years lamp oil was being distilled in large quantities in Pennsylvania. Oil lamps were given glass chimneys and wicks with a spurred-wheel adjustment. Paraffin produced as a by-product of petroleum distillation was used for candles. The 'foot-candle' became the standard of illumination.

The value of coal gas for lighting had first been observed in 1765 by the manager of a coal mine in Whitehaven, on the edge of the

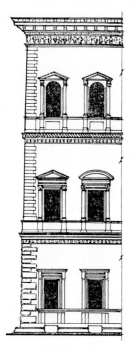

Fig. 5.5.   Windows in the Palazzo Farnese (left) in Rome, designed by Antonio da Sangallo in 1515, and in Lindsey House (right), in Lincoln's Inn Fields, London, built about 1640 and attributed to Inigo Jones.

English Lake District. However, it was not until 1810 that it was used on a significant scale, following the formation of the Gas Light and Coke Company in London. Gas light was no better than oil light until Auer von Welsbach in 1885 invented the incandescent mantle made from fabric impregnated with thorium oxide.

In the meantime electric lighting had been invented. The electric arc light was first used for the South Foreland lighthouse near

Dover in 1858, and arc lights were used for lighting streets and the stages of theatres. However, they were too bright for ordinary artificial lighting. In 1878 and 1879 Joseph Swan in England and Thomas Alva Edison in America invented independently the incandescent electric lamp. They considered litigation over their patent rights, but instead decided to form the Edison and Swan United Electric Light Company, which built the world's first two electric power stations, one in London and one in New York. The use of electric lighting spread rapidly.

It had been observed since the early 18th century that an electric discharge through a rarefied gas produced a glow. In the early 20th century this principle was applied to the manufacture of discharge lamps. It was then noticed that the ultraviolet radiation emitted by many discharge lamps, which was invisible as such, produced visible light if the glass tube was coated with a fluorescent powder. The first fluorescent tubes containing mercury vapour were made commercially in the USA in 1938 and used to light most of the New York World Fair in the same year. Thereafter they were used extensively for lighting offices and factories, because their electricity consumption for the same level of illumination was only about a quarter of that of incandescent lamps, which more than compensated for the higher initial cost. During the 1950s fluorescent tubes largely displaced other forms of lighting in office buildings and factories. In many buildings the length of the standard fluorescent tube became the module for the design of the ceiling, and even of the whole building (Section 6.7). At the same time lighting levels increased greatly. Many architects and their lighting consultants based their design of illumination purely on artificial light, and blocked the admission of natural light where this was necessary to avoid glare. The heat produced by the large number of electric lights in turn increased the air-conditioning load. In the 1970s there was a reaction, leading to increased emphasis on natural lighting.

Actual measurements of daylight were not made prior to the 20th century. In England daylight studies have been based on the daylight factor, which is defined as the ratio of illumination at any point in a room to the illumination at the same instant to a horizontal plane exposed to the unobstructed sky [233]. This depends mainly on the geometry of the building and of any surroundings obstructing the daylight, and on the illumination outside (which can be measured with a lightmeter or taken from a standard table). In America daylight studies have always been based on the actual quantity of light measured at various points in the room.

This difference of approach is largely due to differences in law. English law has recognised the right to 'ancient lights' since medieval times. If a window has been used without interruption for a long time, a term defined in 1832 by a judge as twenty years, the owner of the building acquires a right to prevent the owner of adjoining land from obstructing the light received through that window. In 1922 another judge adopted a daylight factor of 0·2 as the borderline between adequate and inadequate daylight. American courts have not accepted the doctrine of ancient lights.

Model studies have been used for daylight design since the 1930s. The most common type of artificial sky is a hemisphere (Fig. 5.6),

Fig. 5.6.   Model of school room for Ghana, in a hemisphere illuminated by a mixture of incandescent and fluorescent lights to give the distribution of illumination specified for the standard artificial sky. The lighting levels inside the model are measured with the photoelectric cell mounted on a handle.

and in 1942 the Commission Internationale de l'Éclairage (CIE) adopted a proposal by Parry Moon and Domina Eberle Spencer for an international standard sky representing the overcast condition in the temperate zone, which is critical for determining the minimum amount of daylight available [235]. In 1968 the Indian Standards Association adopted a different formula which is particularly useful for the clear blue tropical and sub-tropical sky. Tables and charts have been developed for daylight design [233] and computer programs are now also available.

There is a comfort problem in relation to the luminous environment as there is a comfort problem in relation to thermal environment. Inadequate light was the major problem prior to the 20th century, but this is now easily solved. Glare can result from either daylight or artificial light. It is a fault caused by excessive contrast in luminance within one's field of view [234].

5.6. ACOUSTICS AND NOISE CONTROL

Theatres played an important part in the life of Ancient Greece and, to a lesser extent, of Ancient Rome. Most of our knowledge of their design comes from Vitruvius [11], who set out the proportional relationships in such detail that it is possible to reconstruct the illustrations (Fig. 5.7) which accompanied the original text, but which have not been preserved. Both Greek and Roman theatres had seats arranged in steeply ascending semi-circles. The Greek theatres were generally built into the side of a hill to achieve the necessary slope, but in Roman theatres the banked seats were often backed by high walls. In front of the semi-circles of seats was a flat space, called the *orchestra*; this occupied about three-quarters of a circle (Fig. 5.7) and it was generally paved with polished marble. Behind it was a raised platform, the *proscaenium*, and behind that a heavy solid masonry screen, the *scaena*.

In the Greek theatre the actors performed on the *orchestra*, but in the Roman theatre this space generally was occupied by senators and other dignitaries, and the actors performed on the *proscaenium*.

Vitruvius explained that sound proceeded in expanding concentric circles and emphasised the importance of ascending seats so that

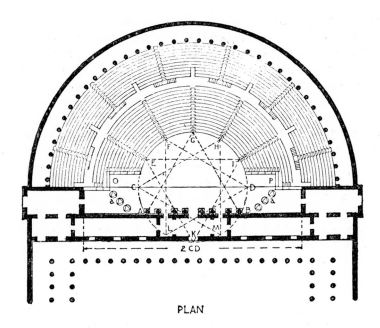

PLAN

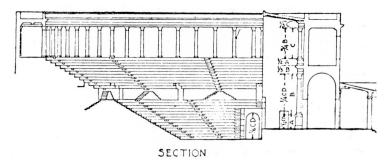

SECTION

Fig. 5.7.   The Roman theatre according to Vitrùvius [11]. The steps between the seats were placed at E, F, G, H and I. There were five openings at the back of the *proscaenium*, through which the actors entered. The six triangles inside circles denoted the *periaktoi*, triangular pieces each decorated with three faces, which could be revolved when the play was to be changed.

every member of the audience received the direct sound. Due to the absence of a roof, the only reflected sound came from the *scaena* and from the unoccupied part of the *orchestra* [237].

Some of the surviving Greek and Roman theatres are very large. The Colosseum in Rome, which was used mainly for gladiatorial performances and is still in reasonable condition, held over 80 000 people. Some others, now in a lesser state of preservation, which *were* used for theatrical performances, may have seated about 20 000 people. The Greeks and the Romans lacked the technology for roofing such large spaces and for providing ventilation for so many people. The lack of a roof to reflect the sound greatly reduced the audibility of the actors. Richardson [238 and 239] thought that the masks worn by Greek actors had an enlarged mouthpiece which acted as a megaphone. Vitruvius [11] mentioned the use of an *echeia*, which he did not fully describe, for reinforcing the sound. This was apparently a vessel or a space under the seats, to whose natural frequency the actor pitched his voice. The actor, however, needed to speak in a monotone, and each actor required his own *echeia*.

When the surviving theatres are used today, electronic sound reinforcement is frequently employed, possibly because modern audiences expect a higher standard of acoustics. However, considering their size, the theatres are remarkably good even without the aid of electronics.

Acoustics received no attention in medieval times. No buildings were designed especially for dramatic performances, and medieval plays were usually performed in the market place. The Gothic cathedrals, which have a high reverberation time, are excellent for the performance of organ music, but it is likely that the organ was designed to fit the cathedral, rather than vice versa. Organs have been used since the 9th century, but the oldest which survives was built in the 14th century.

During the Renaissance there was a return to the Roman type of theatre, but on a much smaller scale. The Teatro Olimpico in Vicenza was designed by Andrea Palladio [15], but completed after his death in 1584. It is a small theatre which differs only in details from the Roman pattern. The back of the proscenium is pierced in the Roman fashion by five openings, but from these radiate seven passages which depict city streets in perspective and actors speaking in these passages behind the proscenium can be heard and seen from most seats. The original theatre had no roof; the present roof is a later addition.

In the Farnese Theatre in Parma, completed by Giovanni Battista Aleotti in 1618, the action took place behind a large opening in the proscenium which could be closed by a curtain. Aleotti's auditorium, which is still in existence, is U-shaped, following the arrangements of the seating customary for the masques held in banquet halls. By the end of the 17th century the banks of seats had become transformed into tiers of boxes and the floor within the horseshoe filled with seats. This remained the pattern for theatres and opera houses until the 20th century. The Scala in Milan (1778), Covent Garden in London (1858), the Staatsoper in Vienna (1869), the Opéra in Paris (1875) and the Metropolitan in New York (1883) all have this type of seating.

Concert halls have a different ancestry. In Mozart's time the largest rooms in which concerts were performed were the ballrooms in which the upper middle classes gathered for social functions. These were generally rectangular rooms with a gallery along three sides, and a platform on the fourth side for the orchestra. When public concerts became common in the late 19th century some of the best concert halls were built on this pattern, for example the Musikvereinsaal in Vienna (1870), St Andrew's Hall in Glasgow (1877), the Concertgebouw in Amsterdam (1888) and the Grosser Tonhallesaal in Zurich (1895). The Boston (Massachusetts) Symphony Hall (1900) differs only in having two galleries. It is still considered one of the world's best concert halls and it was the first whose acoustics were designed in accordance with scientific principles; Wallace Clement Sabine, Professor of Natural Philosophy at Harvard University, was the acoustic consultant.

Sabine made acoustics a quantitative subject. He demonstrated the effect of reflective surfaces and derived a formula for predicting the reverberation time of a hall [241].

In the era between the two World Wars relatively few opera houses and concert halls were built; many cities had already built them during the 19th century and, if some were not notable for their good acoustics, they were too new to warrant replacement. However, thousands of cinemas were erected during that time. Many architects and music lovers regarded them as vulgar, but in later years some were used for symphony concerts with great success. Cinemas built after 1927 were designed for sound films. Many had excellent acoustics, but the problem was much simpler, because the sound was in any case recorded, and it could be adjusted electronically both during production and during reproduction. Within the auditorium there were numerous loudspeakers.

The science of acoustics developed greatly during this period [240 and 242] and it was used in the design of all the concert halls built after 1945. Electronic reinforcement was first used in a concert hall in 1964, when the Royal Festival Hall in London was re-modelled. The hall, built in 1951, was excellent for orchestras of the size used in Mozart's time, but unsatisfactory for music of the late Romantic period. Eighty-nine microphone–amplifier–loudspeaker channels were installed to assist the resonance in the range from 70 to 340 hertz.

The disturbance caused by noise has been a cause of complaint in all large cities from the time of Ancient Rome. The problem has been aggravated in the 20th century by the use of lightweight structures and materials (Section 5.1). Sabine conducted the first tests on sound insulation in 1910 [241], and in 1933 the Acoustical Materials Association was founded in America. The first accurate sound transmission chamber was built at Geneva, Illinois, now the Riverbank Acoustical Laboratories of the Illinois Institute, and data were obtained which proved the mass law. This states that the sound insulation (in decibels) is directly proportional to the logarithm of the weight of the partition per unit area. Extensive data on the sound insulating values of various forms of construction have been established [244], but the problem remains a very difficult one because the current trends towards light construction and mobile partitions run counter to the desiderata for sound insulation [243].

5.7. VERTICAL TRANSPORTATION AND INTERNAL COMMUNICATIONS

Mechanical lifting devices have been used in underground mines at least since Ancient Roman times. In the late 18th century mechanical power produced by water-wheels or steam engines was introduced for hoisting the mining cages, but fatal accidents continued to occur when the cage dropped through failure of the hoisting rope or the mechanical brake. The invention of Elisha Graves Otis therefore consisted not of the invention of the lift, or elevator, but of a safety device which prevented the platform from falling. In 1854 he demonstrated it publicly at the Crystal Palace Exhibition in New York. He had himself hoisted to the ceiling and ordered the rope to be cut; this released a safety catch which engaged ratchets in the guide rails (Fig. 5.8).

The safety lift was immediately adopted in the USA for goods, but its acceptance for passenger transport was initially slow. Only

Fig. 5.8.   Public demonstration of the safety lift by Otis at the Crystal Palace Exhibition in New York in 1854.

one safety passenger lift was built in the next 13 years; it was belt-driven at a speed of 0·2 m/s (40 ft/min). However, by 1870 more than two thousand lifts were in service in America, and all the major buildings erected in Chicago after the Great Fire of 1871 (Section 2.4) had lifts. The limiting factor for the height of buildings had not been the strength of the structure, but the amount of stair-climbing which people were prepared to accept. The lift removed this limitation and Chicago buildings grew in height. By 1882 they had reached ten storeys, and the 'skyscraper' was born. Twenty-one storeys were reached in 1892, 60 storeys in 1913 and 102 storeys in 1931.

The speed and efficiency of lifts also increased rapidly. Hydraulic lifts (Fig. 5.9) were invented in 1878, electric lifts in 1889 and gearless traction in 1903. By the end of the 19th century lift speeds had reached 3·5 m/s (700 ft/min). This equals 13 km/h (8 mph), at that time the speed limit for cyclists in New York streets. Even today it is considered a suitable speed for a lift in a 20-storey building. Control of the lift therefore became more important. The Ward–Leonard multivoltage control was developed in 1892, push-button control in 1893 and automatic control in 1924. This relieved the operator of the need to select the correct acceleration and deceleration, and of drawing the elevator level with the landing. By freeing the operator from the need to make these decisions the speed of operation was approximately doubled.

In 1946 computers were designed for the largest lift installations which coordinated the lifts electronically and adjusted their operation automatically to changes in traffic indicated by the calls made. In 1950 the first lift system was installed which required no attendants to operate it. Lift speeds increased to 9 m/s (1800 ft/min) for buildings of 60 storeys or higher.

Some means of internal communication have been in use for several centuries. Bells operated by pull-wires were used prior to the invention of the electric bell in the late 19th century. Speaking tubes, which are ordinary tubes confining and reflecting the sound, were used before the invention of the telephone in 1875. By 1920 it had become simpler to use a telephone than to walk next door, and inter-office telephones came into general use. In hotels, telephones replaced the array of bells previously required to summon different servants.

Fig. 5.9.   High-speed hydraulic lift installed in the Boreel Building in New York
in 1879.

5.8. THE SIGNIFICANCE OF ELECTRICITY FOR THE DESIGN OF
BUILDINGS

Electricity has perhaps made the single most important contribution to the environmental design of modern buildings, although
all the services could be supplied without electricity. Hydraulic lifts

are still used for some buildings. Communication systems, although limited in speed and versatility, existed before the telephone. Cooking and heating could be done with solid fuel or gas. Fans were driven for a century by steam engines. Artificial light could be produced by oil or gas. However, with the exception of heating, all these services are more efficiently powered by electricity. The ease with which electricity can be supplied through cables in small ducts, without concern for sharp corners or loss of gravity head, and the precise controls made possible through its use, have largely contributed to the present freedom of interior planning and the high quality of the building services.

Electrical phenomena have been studied since the 17th century; the name is derived from the Latin word for amber, which attracts light objects when heated and rubbed. Electric arc light (Section 5.5) was first demonstrated by Humphry Davy at the Royal Institution in 1808. In 1831 Michael Faraday, who succeeded Davy as Professor at the Royal Institution, generated a powerful direct electric current (d.c.) by rotating a copper plate in a short magnetic gap. In 1878 and 1879 Edison and Swan invented the incandescent electric lamp (Section 5.5) and built the first two d.c. power stations, operated by steam engines, in London and in New York to supply the current for their Electric Light Company. Electric light was an immediate success and many more power stations had been built by 1900 to supply the necessary current. Alternating current (a.c.) became generally available in the 1890s and, since it is easier to transmit and to transform it is now generally used.

Thereafter the demand for electric power doubled roughly every twenty years. Until the 1960s this was generally accepted as a desirable improvement in environmental standards, but the energy crisis of the early 1970s (Section 5.4) has led to a greater emphasis on the use of thermal insulation and natural lighting to achieve environmental objectives with less power consumption.

5.9. WATER SUPPLY AND SANITATION

Piped water supplies and sanitary installations have been found in the ruins of several early civilisations, for example in the Palace of

Knossos in Crete, which dates from about 2000 BC [249]. These were, however, only for the use of the ruling family. The Romans created a water supply system which served the entire population. The first of the eleven aqueducts of Ancient Rome, the Appia, was built in 312 BC, and the last in AD 226. By that time the system had a total length of 560 km (350 miles), most of it underground. Since the Romans did not use pressure pipes, the water channels had to cross valleys on embankments or arches for a total length of 80 km (50 miles). These arched aqueducts are still conspicuous objects in the Roman landscape (Fig. 5.10).

Aqueducts were built throughout the Roman Empire, although only a few arches survive. The most notable are El Puente in Segovia, Spain, which still carries water, and the Pont du Gard near Nimes.

Fig. 5.10.   Reconstruction of the crossing of five Roman aqueducts at the Via Latina. The triple aqueduct contained the Marcia, Tepula and Julia and the double aqueduct contained the Claudia and the Anio Novis. The water from the different aqueducts was not allowed to mix. (From a painting by Zeno Diemer in the Deutsches Museum in Munich.)

The Romans did not purify water, but they kept the water from the various aqueducts in separate channels (Fig. 5.10) and protected it from pollution. The cleanest water was used for drinking, and the least satisfactory for sewage disposal and for display, for example, for flooding the Colosseum (Section 5.6) from time to time to stage mock naval battles [246]. By the 2nd century AD there were water supply points throughout the city and the large tenement houses, known as *insulae*, each had their own water supply.

The aqueducts of Rome were maintained in good condition until the 5th century, when the Goths besieged Rome. Thereafter they were gradually destroyed and the water supply failed completely in the 11th century. In the 17th century three of the aqueducts were restored; these still form part of the water supply system of modern Rome.

The *thermae* (public baths) of Rome were among its most magnificent buildings. They contained a cold bath, sometimes a hot bath, rooms for exercise, and rooms heated by hypocausts (Fig. 5.4) which performed a function similar to that of a modern Turkish bath. Thermae were built all over the Roman Empire, for example at Bath in England.

Water-borne sewerage existed on a small scale before Roman times; sometimes, as in Knossos, by building a latrine over a running brook; sometimes, as in Niniveh, by using jugs of water. During the Roman Empire latrines with running water were supplied for most of the population [247]. The sewage of Rome was discharged through the *Cloaca Maxima* in the River Tiber.

Medieval standards of hygiene fell far below those of Ancient Rome. In London the River Thames and wells provided the only water supply until the 13th century when a pipe was laid from Tyburn (where the Marble Arch now stands). By the early 19th century there were nine water supply companies which supplied piped water, but the purity varied greatly.

Cesspools for sewage disposal were reasonably effective for small communities. However, in cities they polluted rivers and wells, and the pollution of water supplies remained a problem from the fall of the Roman Empire to the 19th century. Epidemics were frequent and virulent. In 1853 John Snow traced an outbreak of cholera to the pollution of a particular well by a nearby cesspool [248].

A few years earlier Edwin Chadwick had produced a report [250] which contrasted unfavourably the sanitary conditions of contemporary Britain with those of Ancient Rome. This led to the construction of the London Main Drainage Scheme in 1856, and to an Act passed in 1875 which required local authorities in Britain to build sewerage works. Once the sewage had been removed, purification of the water drawn from wells and rivers through sand filters became practicable.

The first modern aqueduct was the Old Croton Aqueduct [252], opened in 1842, which provided New York City with all the clean water it needed. In 1847 the Manchester Town Council built the Longdendale Reservoir in Derbyshire. These water supplies drawn from a clean source and conveyed through closed channels marked a return to the water supply system of Ancient Rome and, until water purification was perfected in the 20th century, they were superior to the water supply of London, drawn from rivers and wells.

Water closets (WC's) were invented in England in the late 18th century. The earliest types were difficult to keep clean. In the 1870s Thomas William Twyford, a potter in Hanley, produced 'washout closets' consisting of a single piece of glazed earthenware without moving parts [249]. These WC's were similar to the type still in use today. Water closets removed the sewage from the house without the inconvenience associated with the carting of night soil, but the sanitary problem remained until sewage disposal plants were developed towards the end of the 19th century.

Water closets required soil drains, and once these had been installed it became common to connect kitchen sinks and bath tubs to them; portable baths filled by hand and emptied by hand had been in use by the upper and middle classes since the 18th century. By 1870 baths with running water were common in the houses of the wealthy and by 1910 they were common in British working-class houses. In the early 20th century well-to-do Americans started to provide individual bathrooms for each bedroom, a practice only gradually copied in Europe.

The introduction of piped water and sewerage had a profound effect on the design of buildings. In multistorey buildings it became necessary to arrange bathrooms, kitchens and WC's on top of one another, since the soil drains required an adequate fall and gentle bends. In due course these rooms, which had previously been the cheapest part of the building, became the most expensive.

5.10. FIRE PREVENTION

Fire has been, and still is, a far greater destroyer of buildings and their occupants than structural failure. From the earliest times fires were started by firebrands thrown by a besieging army. In recent years aerial bombardment has had a similar effect. The firestorm following the air raid on Dresden in 1945 destroyed most of the city, and killed approximately 35 000 people. Earthquakes were often followed by fire; about 600 people died in the earthquake and fire of San Francisco in 1906, but approximately 100 000 people are estimated to have been killed by the fire following the Tokyo earthquake of 1923.

By comparison, man-made fires have often killed relatively few people, even though they have caused great material damage. The Great Fire which destroyed most of London in 1666 took only six lives, because the fire spread slowly over a period of several days. Some modern fires have caused great material loss; for example the damage due to a fire in the covered bazaars of Istanbul in 1954 was estimated at about 100 million pounds sterling.

Lightning was a major cause of fire in important public buildings until Benjamin Franklin invented the lightning conductor in 1750. Lightning tends to strike the highest point, and in flat country classical temples, Gothic cathedrals and Renaissance domes therefore attracted lightning. It was highly probable that a fire would be started in a tall wooden roof by lightning over a period of several centuries.

The temples of Ancient Greece normally had timber roofs, but in the Hellenistic period stone roofs became common. Alberti [14] reported Julius Caesar as saying that Alexandria survived his siege because most of the important buildings were roofed with masonry vaults.

The cross-vaulted roofs of the Gothic cathedrals required a pitched timber roof to protect them from rain. In turn the masonry vaults prevented the spread of fire from the timber roof. Thus the double roof structure (Fig. 1.4) which at first sight seems wasteful, had an essential protective function.

Except during the Roman Empire, fire fighting was limited by the water supply, and by difficulties of delivering the water to the seat of the fire; this was usually done by passing buckets from hand to hand. However, Roman settlements generally had ample water and some had cylinder pumps for fire fighting [148].

Both in Ancient Roman and in medieval times, burning timber was pulled off the roof with long-handled hooks and houses were demolished in the path of the fire to create a firebreak. After the Great Fire of AD 64, the Emperor Nero cut several wide straight roads through Rome which acted as firebreaks and provided quick access by fire-fighters; the modern Via del Corso is one of them. After the passing of the Roman Empire the breakdown in security required that people be crowded inside the protecting walls of the city; this greatly complicated fire protection. However, the problem remained even after the development of artillery had made the walls obsolete. Christopher Wren (Section 1.5) failed after the Fire of 1666 where Nero had succeeded. Because of disputes over property rights the City of London was rebuilt with the narrow main roads originally laid out for a small Roman provincial city 15 centuries earlier.

The Great Fire of London led to the creation of the first modern fire brigades. In 1680 Nicholas Barbon, a London builder, offered to insure buildings against fire; to protect them he created his own professional fire brigade, which confined itself to extinguishing fires in the houses owned by the subscribers. Other private fire brigades soon followed. The London insurance companies combined their fire brigades into a single service only in 1832. Many European and American cities created full-time fire brigades in the 18th century, mostly operated by the government.

Fire engines which pumped water through leather hoses had already been in use at the time of London fire of 1666. During the 18th century these became more powerful and up to 50 people were used to operate the hand-pumps. The first steam-operated fire engines were built in New York in the early 19th century. Most of these were drawn at great speed by teams of horses and the first self-propelled steam-operated fire engines were no faster. Sectional ladders were already used in medieval times. Self-supporting extending ladders came into use during the middle of the 19th century [1]. In the late 19th and the first half of the 20th century, the height of buildings was limited in many cities by the length of the fire brigade's longest extending ladder. This was generally 43 m (141 ft).

When the first tall buildings were erected, it became clear that fire-fighting would have to be done within the building instead of relying on the fireman poised outside on a self-supporting ladder. Thus fire-resistant construction, firestairs, sprinklers and alarm systems became more important [150].

Several automatic water extinguishing systems were in use in the first half of the 19th century. In one of these the fire burned a combustible cord supporting a weight which opened a spring-operated valve. Water then flowed from a large number of nozzles; this extinguished the fire, but the resulting water damage was often greater than that caused by the fire. In 1874 Henry S. Parmalee invented automatic sprinklers fitted to each of the water nozzles. The fire fused a link to release the water spray; the sprinklers were therefore opened only where the temperature was high enough.

Fire alarms were introduced in the 1860s. They were operated by the thermal expansion of a spring or a mercury column which closed an electric circuit to sound a bell. Later, an electric alarm was also set off at the nearest fire station. Modern fire detectors utilise both the rise in temperature and the smoke produced by a fire; the latter can be detected by measuring the loss of light from a beam falling on a photoelectric cell.

Fire-resistant construction remains, however, the single most effective means of reducing the risk of fire. It was the main reason for the use of masonry materials, rather than the structurally more versatile timber and thus, from ancient times until the 18th century, for the use of arches, vaults and domes (Section 1.2). It was also a principal reason for the use of cast iron as the structural material for factories in the 19th century (Section 2.2).

In addition various methods have been used, at least since Ancient Roman times, to increase the fire resistance of timber. Timber chars during combustion and the charcoal so produced is an insulator. Thus large pieces of timber have much greater fire resistance than small pieces. This can be further improved by painting the timber with a fire-retarding liquid which solidifies on drying. Roman assault batteries were so treated. The principal substances used until the 19th century were borax, alum and ferrous sulphate.

Timber could also be protected by a sheet of metal (bronze or iron), or by a coat of stucco mixed from lime or plaster of Paris and sand, reinforced with hair or dried grass [146].

The actual floor structure spanning between the loadbearing beams presented a greater problem. The most effective method was to use jack arches (Section 2.2) of brick or concrete with concrete fillers; these could be made lighter and more fireproof by casting hollow pots into the concrete. This method was used in Ancient Rome; it was revived in France and in England in the 18th century. A simpler, but less effective method was to protect the timber planks with a plaster ceiling underneath and a composition floor above.

Cast iron girders and columns were fire-resistant up to a temperature of about 550°C (1020°F), because the material is brittle and consequently does not creep as much as steel. However, when steel was substituted for cast iron in the late 19th century, additional fireproofing was required, because steel deflects dangerously at temperatures above 450°C (840°F), which are easily attained in large fires. This was at first provided by a protective cover of rectangular hollow tiles, but these performed poorly in the fire following the San Francisco earthquake of 1906 [149]. Later building regulations specified that the tiles should be closely fitting, or alternatively that not less than 50 mm (2 in) of solid concrete, or a lightweight fireproofing consisting of gypsum on metal lath (or more recently sprayed vermiculite) be used.

5.11. THE INTEGRATED DESIGN OF BUILDING SERVICES

The growing complexity of the services and of the functional problems of the building envelope raised problems of integration. In traditional construction the chimney always formed part of the architect's design and drains had to be installed during construction; however, electric conduits, water pipes and gas pipes were not always located during design; holes were frequently cut for them in the completed fabric of the building and then made good.

This is not feasible with many modern materials and dry methods of construction, where both cutting and making good are more difficult. Furthermore, the greatly increased number of locations for electric light and power, and the large volume occupied by air-conditioning ducts, made integrated planning of the services during the initial stages of the design of tall buildings essential in the 1950s. One of the arguments in favour of modular coordination and industrialised building methods was the greater measure of control possible in standardised sub-assemblies.

Electrical services, vertical transportation and communication systems are the inevitable by-product of high-density living. Air conditioning is not essential in many large cities, but the experience of Sydney, at any rate, has shown that a luxury can quickly become a necessity. In 1950 rentable air-conditioned offices were non-existent; by 1964 only air-conditioned offices were built for tenancies in new city buildings, because no property owner in the city expected to be able to let offices without air conditioning at an economical rental.

The functional efficiency of the fabric of the building should be fully considered in the design of the building services, although at the time of writing (1975) this is still exceptional. The shielding of the walls and windows from the sun affects both the lighting and the heating (or cooling) of the building. Noise control is affected by ventilation, both through windows and through ducts; by the design of the partitions, particularly if they are movable, and of the outside walls; and by the arrangement of the services in a false ceiling.

This is a complex task and it may reasonably be asked why we have abandoned solid masonry buildings, which gave generally good sound insulation and, in temperate climates, provided an adequate thermal capacity to produce satisfactory indoor conditions in all but the hottest weather without artificial cooling. At least part of the answer lies in the need to build high in cities which are constantly growing more populous.

The limit of the loadbearing wall was reached in 1889 when the Monadnock Building in Chicago required solid loadbearing walls 1·8 m (6 ft) thick, to reach a height of sixteen floors [54]. With a skeleton frame this could be reduced to less than 0·3 m (1 ft), irrespective of height. However, in the last two decades there has been a revival of brick walls for multi-storey buildings, because of the economy achieved by using loadbearing walls which also provide substantial insulation. In the 1950s new methods for their design were developed which took account of the wind resistance offered by cross-walls and floor slabs. Buildings of up to 21 storeys have now been built with brick walls only 0·4 m (1 ft 4 in) thick without skeleton frames [179].

Chapter 6

Building Materials, and the Industrialisation of Building

When people agree with me, I always fear that I must be wrong.

Oscar Wilde

6.1. MASONRY MATERIALS

Natural stone was the principal material for important buildings up to the 20th century, because it is attractive in appearance and fire resistant. Stone can be very durable (Fig. 6.1). However, in some medieval cathedrals the cost of the repairs due to erosion has greatly exceeded the original cost of the masonry fabric and some recent buildings have also needed extensive maintenance; two such examples from the mid-19th century are the Palace of Westminster (the Houses of Parliament) and the Great Hall of the University of Sydney, Australia.

Although some quarries have become depleted, many famous stones are still obtainable, for example, the Pentelic marble used for the Parthenon, the travertine employed in Ancient Rome, the Carrara marble favoured by Michelangelo and the Portland stone which was chosen for St Paul's Cathedral.

There is no imminent danger of a shortage of natural stone and the replacement of natural stone by concrete in the mid-20th century was mainly due to the rapid increase in the cost of labour.

Concrete has an earlier history (Section 2.6); it had become the principal material for important structures in Ancient Rome by the 2nd century AD. Their exterior faces (Section 2.6) were almost invariably cast against permanent formwork of brick, or sometimes of natural stone [113–117]. Exposed concrete was visible only in some parts of the interior. It is unlikely that this was due to problems of providing wooden formwork capable of withstanding the pressure of the liquid concrete, because in large structures the *caementa* (large

Fig. 6.1.   Carvings on the natural stone facing for a staircase at Persepolis,
Iran, cut in the 5th century BC and still perfectly distinct.

pieces of aggregate) were placed before the liquid mortar was cast
(Section 2.6) and were thus mostly self-supporting; the Romans were
also quite capable of building wooden structures for military purposes which resisted horizontal forces. It is more probable that they
faced concrete structures with brick or stone veneer because their
aesthetics was conservative and because they had difficulty in
producing an attractive surface finish on concrete.

    This was still a major problem when concrete construction was
resumed in the early 19th century (Section 2.6). A number of purely
functional structures were built with exposed concrete. However,

while many of the 'no-nonsense' factory buildings of that time built with natural stone are today regarded as fine examples of functional architecture, the concrete buildings of the same period are considered interesting rather than beautiful. A number of Neo-Gothic churches and some Neo-Classical residences were built in concrete in the middle of the 19th century, which also suffered from the poor quality of the surface finish.

In 1891 Ransome achieved an acceptable finish on the classical facade of the Stanford Museum (Section 2.7) by removing the cement film through tooling and exposing the aggregate.

Auguste Perret used exposed concrete from 1905 onwards and many of his buildings are still admired for the high quality of the finish. This was produced partly by precasting and partly by showing the timber grain of carefully made formwork.

Frank Lloyd Wright also employed concrete from 1905 onwards and achieved a good finish by using precast units as permanent formwork for site-cast concrete. Other architects of the modern school were less successful in their use of exposed concrete during the 1920s and 1930s and some buildings which looked excellent when new have weathered badly.

All but one of the principal methods of surface finish in use today were known, in principle, in 1900: showing the board marks left by the timber formwork; using enamelled steel forms to produce a glazed finish; removing the cement by brushing, acid treatment, sand-blasting or bush-hammering; pressing specially selected aggregate into the wet concrete surface to produce a decorative exposed aggregate; and applying various patterns to the concrete to detract attention from surface blemishes. Only white cement was a later development. The lack of success of these methods, except when used by a few skilled people, was due to insufficient experimentation and attention to detail. When exposed concrete became an economic necessity in the 1950s, the quality of its finish improved rapidly.

Brick is the principal material of the structures surviving from Ancient Mesopotamia, where natural stone and timber were scarce. It was used extensively in Ancient Rome. In medieval Europe, brickmaking was not as well-developed and brick was used mainly in regions where suitable natural stone was not available, such as North Germany, The Netherlands and East England [49]. At the same time bricklaying in intricate patterns became an art form in Muslim countries, particularly in Turkey, Iran and southern Russia.

From the 15th century onwards brick manufacture improved in northern Europe. Brick became gradually cheaper than natural stone and it was preferred for a wide range of buildings for this reason. When the Industrial Revolution created a need for a vast number of new houses in the early 19th century, brick became the principal building material.

From the technical point of view, bricks present fewer problems of durability than natural stone. If they are well-burnt, they are unlikely to disintegrate due to weathering; since they are manufactured, their performance is more predictable than that of material taken from a quarry. Roman and medieval bricks generally had a thickness ranging from 40 to 60 mm ($1\frac{1}{2}$ to $2\frac{1}{4}$ in), because of the difficulty of firing thicker bricks without distortion. In the 17th century the thickness increased and the standard English brick became $9 \times 4\frac{1}{2} \times 3$ in ($231 \times 115 \times 77$ mm).

It weighed a little over 3 kg (about 7 lb), and it could easily be lifted by a bricklayer with one hand. In the 20th century experiments were carried out to determine the appropriate size for a masonry unit for prefabricated construction. Assuming that the units are to be joined by mortar and the work done by one man, the brick has almost ideal dimensions and weight. This is one reason why brickwork has remained economical when other traditional methods of construction became uncompetitive (Section 6.8).

6.2. Metals

No metals were employed in the building industry before the 19th century which had not been known to the Ancient World. Iron and bronze (an alloy of copper and tin) were used for clamps, dowels and door hinges at least 3000 years ago. Copper and lead were employed as roofing materials. The Romans made water-pipes of lead; the Byzantines used it to cement the masonry of the piers of St Sophia (Section 1.3).

A great quantity of bronze was used both inside and outside the

Pantheon in Rome (Fig. 1.1) in the 2nd century AD. The gold-plated bronze tiles covering the roof outside were removed to Constantinople by the Emperor Constans II in the 7th century; the bronze girders holding up the portico and the bronze covering the inside of the dome remained until the reign of Pope Urban VIII in the 17th century, when they were used for Bernini's baldachino in St Peter's [86], and the remainder turned into eighty cannons for the Castel Sant'Angelo.

Wrought iron tie bars were used occasionally in Byzantine and Gothic architecture, and frequently in Muslim architecture, in place of buttresses. In the Duomo of Florence (Fig. 1.7) lead-covered iron clamps were used in the 15th century to join the blocks of stone forming the 'stone chains', and tin-plated iron bolts were used to join the pieces of timber forming the 'timber chain'. Leone Battista Alberti [14] in the same century recommended the use of brass (an alloy of copper and zinc) for clamps in marble, because of the danger of staining when iron was used. Wrought iron chains were used to restrain the hoop tension both in St Peter's Basilica in Rome and in St Paul's Cathedral in London (Section 1.5).

Cast iron had been known in China in ancient times, but in Europe it was discovered only in the 15th century [106]. It remained an expensive material until the early 18th century, when coke was first produced and the size of blast furnaces, which had previously used charcoal, could be increased. In the late 18th century iron technology made great advances, the price of both cast and wrought iron fell sharply, and it began to be used as a structural material (Section 2.2).

Steel was a very scarce and valuable material in the ancient and medieval world [64]. Except for the rare cast Wootz steel of India, it was made from wrought iron laboriously hammered in a forge to increase the carbon content and distribute it evenly through the metal [105]. One obstacle to its cheaper production was the belief, already held by Aristotle, that steel was a particularly pure form of iron, purified by prolonged hammering in the fire to drive out its impurities. Until the 19th century (Section 2.2) steel remained too expensive to be used as a building material.

Stainless steel was invented independently in England, Germany and the USA in the early 20th century. There are several alloys of iron which do not rust; all contain at least 10% chromium and most also contain some nickel.

The first prominent architectural use of stainless steel was in the Chrysler Building, New York, whose tower was sheathed in the metal in 1929. In 1932 the column and mullion covers of the Empire State Building were made from it. The first stainless steel curtain wall was manufactured in 1948 for the General Electric turbine building, Schenectady, a four-storey structure, and in 1951 the entire surface of the 24-storey Gateway Center in Pittsburgh was covered with 22-gauge stainless steel, with relatively small windows.

Aluminium was the first of the new metals. Its name derives from alum (a double sulphate of aluminium and potassium), the alumen used by the Romans in the dyeing trade. Humphry Davy produced in 1809 an aluminium–iron alloy by electrolysis; but the Danish scientist Hans Christian Oersted in 1825 was the first to separate the metal. In 1845 Friedrich Wöhler in Germany produced enough aluminium to determine its density and physical properties; however, it remained a rarity until Paul Louis Héroult in France and Charles Martin Hall in America, working independently, in 1886 developed the commercial process still in use today. The *Encyclopaedia Britannica* [1] in 1875 described aluminium as a metal used in jewellery and, because of its light weight, in balance beams. In 1893 Eros statue in Piccadilly Circus, London, was made from aluminium. One of the earliest architectural uses was as an ornamental sheet metal cornice on the Canada Life Insurance Building in Montreal in 1896, and the first corrugated aluminium roof was laid on the Chief Secretary's Office in Macquarie Street, Sydney, in 1900. The sheets had been fixed with copper nails (a mistake frequently made for many years thereafter although the electrochemical series of metals was well known at the time), which produced holes in the aluminium; however, the sheets were otherwise in excellent condition when replaced in 1937.

Because of the high chemical reactivity of aluminium, the durability conferred by the hard oxide skin was not appreciated at first and high price limited its use until the 1930s. In 1932 cast aluminium spandrels were used in the Rockefeller Center, New York, and in 1936 Giles Scott used aluminium windows and doors for the Cambridge University Library. During World War II, world production of aluminium almost quadrupled and the building industry absorbed a large part of the surplus after the war.

The experience gained with the production of aircraft and the urgent need for housing led to the manufacture of complete metal houses. These houses were not economical at the time and they did not meet with popular approval (Section 6.6); neither did the lightness of aluminium compensate for its high price in ordinary structural applications. There have, however, been a few notable architectural structures, for example the Dome of Discovery (Section 4.7) in 1951 and the Myer Music Bowl (Fig. 4.12) in 1957 which utilised aluminium.

Aluminium windows can compete with steel windows because the complicated shapes can be produced cheaply by extruding the hot aluminium alloy through a die. Aluminium windows do not require painting, they are attractive in appearance and they are much lighter than steel windows [190]. Aluminium roof sheets can compete with steel for longer spans.

Aluminium has become the most widely used material for metal curtain walls since Wallace K. Harrison first employed it for the trim of the United Nations Secretariat in New York in 1950 and for the entire facade of the Alcoa Building in Pittsburgh in 1953 (Fig. 6.2). For external applications aluminium is usually anodised, *i.e.* the thickness of the naturally formed aluminium oxide skin is increased electrochemically to improve the weathering quality. It is possible to colour the oxide skin during this process. In the 1950s organic colours were used which subsequently faded; the colours for external use are now always inorganic and permanent.

Copper, brass and bronze, in addition to their traditional use, have also been used for curtain walls, but only on a limited scale, because aluminium can be anodised to give a similar appearance for less cost.

6.3. GLASS

The manufacture of glass by fusing soda-ash and sand is of very ancient origin. Exquisitely made glass jewellery has been found in the tombs of the pharaohs, and 'glasses' for drinking were known in

Fig. 6.2.   Alcoa Building in Pittsburgh, faced with stamped aluminium panels 4·4 mm ($\frac{1}{8}$ in) thick, backed with 100 mm (4 in) of lightweight perlite concrete for insulation. It was designed by Wallace K. Harrison in 1953.

antiquity. However, glass was little used as a building material. Vitruvius [11] who described every single material in detail did not mention it. A few window panes have been found, for example in the buried city of Pompeii, but glazed windows were rare in Ancient Rome.

Windows became more common during the Middle Ages. The best-known examples are the stained glass windows of the Gothic cathedrals, painted since the 12th century. From the 14th century onwards glass windows were frequently used in palaces, and in the 16th century they became common in middle-class houses.

In Britain the northern latitude and the overcast skies had always made large windows desirable (Fig. 5.5) and, during the peaceful reign of Elizabeth I, the size of windows increased even for private buildings.

Some medieval and Renaissance buildings have very large windows; few modern public buildings have continuous glazed surfaces comparable in size to the west window of a Gothic cathedral and few modern residences have windows as large as those of Hardwick Hall, built in Derbyshire in the 1590s.

Since it was impossible to make large panes of glass, the individual glass pieces were usually assembled into larger units with lead cames. These were made into still larger units with iron bars varnished to protect them from rust. These assemblies of glass and metal were then attached to stone mullions and transoms.

Roman and medieval glass was probably made by the cylinder process described by the Benedictine monk Theophilus in the 10th century [192]. The liquid glass was blown into a large bulb, which was given a cylindrical form by rotating it. Both ends of the cylinder were pierced and the openings widened to the general diameter of the cylinder. The cylinder was annealed, then split longitudinally with red-hot iron shears. It was next reheated on the bed of the oven (Fig. 6.3) and flattened into a sheet.

The resulting glass had many imperfections. It generally contained air bubbles and, if there were too many of these, it became translucent rather than transparent. This was at least partly the reason for the practice of staining, that is, painting the windows of churches. On the other hand, the air bubbles gave the colours of the stained glass a brilliance which the more perfect glass of the 19th century lacked, and in the Neo-Gothic era special 'antique' glass was made to imitate the appearance of medieval glass.

The transparency of glass improved greatly when the crown-glass process was perfected. Crown glass was made by blowing the liquid glass into a globe, then spinning it until the centrifugal force gave it a wheel-like shape. This method had been used in Syria in ancient times and in Venice small round crown-glass panes were made in the

Fig. 6.3. Final stage in the manufacture of cylinder glass. The cylinder of glass has been pierced at its ends and split longitudinally. It is then reheated and flattened into a sheet. (From Ref. 192.)

Middle Ages. In the 15th century Venetian glass blowers blew the glass into larger and thinner discs, up to 1·4 m (4 ft 7 in) in diameter (Fig. 6.4). The discs were then cut up into rectangular pieces. Since it did not come into contact with the furnace or any other surface during manufacture, crown glass had a freedom from surface defects and a clarity which could not be achieved with cylinder glass. The crown-glass process was brought to England by Venetian glass blowers in the 16th century. The first recorded use of crown glass for windows was in 1685, when the original windows in Inigo Jones's Banqueting House in Whitehall were replaced with balanced sliding

Fig. 6.4.   The process of crown-glass making illustrated in William Cooper's
Crown-Glass Cutter and Glazier's Manual, 1825. (From Ref. 1.)

sash windows [191]. Christopher Wren used similar windows for the
new palace at Hampton Court. The slightly curved, brilliantly clear
crown glass fitted into sliding window sashes remained a popular
material in Britain until the 19th century.

In the early 19th century the cylinder process was greatly improved in France and in 1832 Lucas Chance began to use the French
process in his Birmingham works. The cylinder was blown larger
and allowed to cool. Instead of being cut hot with iron shears, it
was cut cold with a diamond cutter, reheated and flattened out on a
bed of smooth glass, instead of an iron plate covered with sand. With
the new process a better surface finish and larger sheets could be
produced.

In 1904 Emile Fourcault in Belgium and in 1905 the Libby–Owens
Glass Company in the USA developed processes for drawing sheet
glass directly from a pool of molten glass.

These innovations were essential for the new uses of glass. The
Crystal Palace (Section 6.6) could not have been built without the
improved cylinder process, nor could the glass-walled buildings of
the 1920s have been erected without the Fourcault process.

In the early 18th century orangeries became fashionable in northern Europe. These were garden houses with large windows facing south, for growing orange trees and other plants which required protection from the cold in winter. In the 19th century complete glass houses were built for the same reason (Fig. 6.5).

Fig. 6.5.   Interior of the Conservatory at the Horticultural Gardens in Chiswick, 1841. (From *London*, edited by Charles Knight and published by Knight & Co., London 1842.)

The Crystal Palace (Section 6.6 and Fig. 6.8) was, in fact, a large greenhouse. It in turn provided the prototype for later glass-walled exhibition buildings, such as the Galerie des Machines (Section 2.2), and for the newly established department stores which, prior to the development of electric lighting, depended on glass-roofed internal light wells (Section 5.5), as did the 19th-century shopping arcades.

In the 20th century there was no longer any need to depend on glass for lighting, and the new glass-walled buildings thus had an aesthetic, rather than a functional justification: their clean, manufactured appearance appealed to the pioneers of modern architecture. Walter Gropius used glass walls in two factories in Germany in 1911 and 1914 and the glass wall of his *Bauhaus* in Dessau, built in 1926, extended without a break through three floors. Ludwig Mies van der Rohe and Le Corbusier also used large glass surfaces in many of their buildings before 1945.

In the late 1940s and the 1950s the concept of a light structural frame, and the new technology of air conditioning (Section 5.1 and 5.4) combined to produce the sealed glass curtain wall. This was an immediate success in America, France and West Germany, where it is still used extensively for tall buildings. Heat-absorbing glass, heat-reflecting glass, and double glazing were employed after 1950 to reduce the cooling loads, together with lightweight thermal insulation in the non-transparent portions of the wall. In sub-tropical and tropical regions sunshading devices were frequently included in the design, or installed afterwards.

Most countries, even those of Eastern Europe, have built glass-walled buildings, but in some it was a passing phase, to be succeeded by curtain walls made from materials with better insulating properties, such as precast concrete.

6.4. PLASTICS AND ADHESIVES

Plastics are materials which can be formed plastically at moderate temperatures, much below those required for softening metals or glass, but which turn hard at normal temperatures. Asphalt found in Mesopotamia was known to the Ancient Assyrians. It was used as a waterproofing material and as a masonry cement in the Roman and

Byzantine Empires. Shellac, a natural resin made from incrustations on certain trees by an insect, was imported from India and much used in the 18th and 19th centuries.

The first synthetic resins were produced in the 1860s to provide a cheaper and more plentiful alternative to natural ivory and horn. In 1865 Alexander Parkes produced in England parkesine from nitrocellulose and camphor. Commercially more successful was celluloid, produced in the USA in 1869 by John Wyatt from the same materials; it was, however, highly flammable. In 1927 Otto Roehm in Germany made another transparent, but safer product by polymerising methyl methacrylate; this is now marketed under the names Perspex and Plexiglas. During World War II numerous new plastics were developed, notably in the USA and in Germany, as substitutes for scarce materials and, after the war, plastics replaced metals and timber for many traditional uses [193]. Plastics proved particularly suitable for hard-wearing surfaces in kitchens and offices, for floor finishes, for suspended ceilings and for lightweight insulating materials. Plastics have been the principal material for pneumatic structures (Section 4.8), but complete houses built from plastics have remained in the experimental stage at the time of writing (1975).

Synthetic plastics have replaced traditional vehicles in most paints [194]. They have also largely replaced traditional glues made from bones, fish waste and casein, particularly for exterior applications which must be waterproof. The joints of curtain walls made of metal, glass or concrete could not have been sealed satisfactorily without synthetic plastics, neither could waterproof plywood or particle board have been produced.

6.5. TIMBER

Timber is the most widely used of all the traditional building materials. Its supply is inexhaustible, provided it is replenished by re-afforestation. Timber can be economically transported by ship over long distances. In some countries the building industry relies almost entirely on imported timber.

The oldest timber structures which survive date from the Middle

Ages. Most have mortise-and-tenon joints or dovetail joints, which required a great deal of labour. In the 19th century the mass production of nails led to much cheaper methods of jointing. In 1833 George Washington Snow built the first balloon frame for a church in Chicago; this employed only nailed joints and used timber studs which were smaller and more closely spaced than those of traditional construction. The name 'balloon frame', given because of the lightness of the structure, was originally a term of ridicule, but the technique soon spread to most parts of America and to Australia.

The new construction method greatly reduced the amount of labour needed for building timber houses. In due course it was used also for the 'brick-veneer' house, which is a timber-framed house lined inside with a wood composition board or a gypsum board and outside with a single leaf of brickwork. It looks like a brick house and the outer leaf protects the timber frame in the event of an exterior fire, such as a bush fire.

The susceptibility of timber to destruction by fire, fungi, borers and termites had become less of a problem by the beginning of the 20th century because of better methods of fire fighting and pest control. However, its low strength *across* the grain and its variable strength due to knots, gum pockets and sloping grain remained disadvantages. Both were overcome by using several laminates of timber with the grain at right angles in alternative laminates; the effect of grain direction was thus eliminated and any defect confined to a single laminate. Structural plywood was patented by Otto Hetzer in Germany in 1905, using a casein glue. Phenol formaldehyde was the first synthetic resin employed to produce a waterproof plywood for exterior use, but since the acid hardener required attacks some species of timber, urea formaldehyde is now the most common type. The difference between veneering an inferior timber with a high-quality surface, a technique already known to the Ancient Egyptians, and a laminated plywood lies in the strength of the modern product.

Large pieces of timber have, in the past, been difficult to obtain, because large trees are rare and take hundreds of years to grow; however, there is no limit to the size which can be produced by lamination. Curved structures can also be made with ease by gluing the individual laminates after they have been bent to shape (Fig. 6.6).

Plastic binders are also the basis of wood composition board.

Fig. 6.6.   Eagle Aviary at the Bristol Zoo, England (Architects: Saxon, Smith and Partners, Chester.) Curved members are easily produced in laminated timber.

Some wood chips are made from fully grown trees, but a proportion is produced from industrial offcuts, from pieces left over when round trees are converted into rectangular sections, and from small trees cut to thin out a stand of timber. The chips are cemented with a suitable synthetic resin, such as urea formaldehyde. Depending on their density, composition boards can be used as thermal insulating materials; as particle boards for cupboards, partitions and ceilings; or as hardboards for walls and ceilings requiring greater strength. These materials can be produced in large sheets and they are related to natural timber as concrete is related to natural stone.

6.6. Prefabrication and System Building

Timber houses have been prefabricated in panels at least since the 17th century, when they were taken in this form from England to North America. In the following century similar panels were made on the American east coast for shipping to the West Indies.

Cast iron and wrought iron houses were prefabricated in Britain for export from the early 1830s to the middle 1850s. Their main destinations were Australia, the West Indies and California.

In 1849, the second year of the gold rush, prefabricated houses of timber and iron arrived in California not merely from England and the American east coast, but also from Australia and New Zealand.

In each case the reason for the import of prefabricated houses lay in the difficulty of building them to a satisfactory standard from local materials.

Prefabricated concrete [197] had a different reason. It has been made since the 1890s (Fig. 6.7), because of the difficulty of accurately predicting the strength of concrete structures at the time. The strength of site-cast concrete can only be determined by theory, and the theory was not then well developed (Section 2.7). However, the strength of precast concrete could be ascertained by testing it to destruction, after which identical parts were then prefabricated. By 1910 the theory of reinforced concrete design was much improved, but in the 1920s precast concrete had a revival for system building, *i.e.* the construction of buildings from a restricted number of standard components.

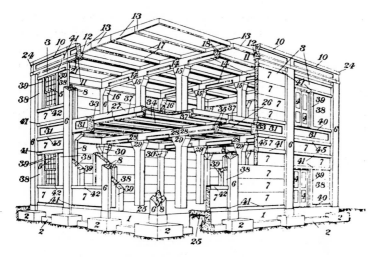

Fig. 6.7. Completely precast concrete building system patented by John E. Conzelman in the USA in 1912. (From Ref. 197.)

The Crystal Palace [195 and 196], prefabricated and erected in Hyde Park, London, in a mere nine months in 1850–51, was the first large system building. It was assembled almost entirely from a few standardised parts. There were only three sizes of truss and the connections were also standardised. All the window glass, made by Lucas Chance (Section 6.3), was of one standard size. The erection procedure (Fig. 6.8) was mechanised, even though the machine was operated by horsepower. It was only by this high degree of mechanisation and standardisation that the building could have been built in the short time which remained between the decision of the Commissioners for the Exhibition to accept the design and the advertised opening date of the exhibition.

In the second half of the 19th century standardisation and mass production were applied to a wide variety of manufactures. The movement started in the USA where labour was scarce and expensive, but it soon spread to Europe. By 1900 the cost of mass-produced clothes had become much cheaper than those made individually in small workshops and most working people wore them; by 1925, so did most gentlemen. It was reasonable to assume that similar

Fig. 6.8.   Erection in the late autumn of 1850 of the structure of the Crystal Palace, designed by Joseph Paxton and the construction firm of Fox and Henderson to house the world's first international exhibition. The cast iron girders were lifted by horsepower. The glazing wagons (six are shown near the top of this engraving) were pulled along by mechanisms operated by two men. (From Ref. 195.)

advantages could be derived from the production of mass-produced standardised housing.

It is worth noting that housing in the 18th and 19th century was already to a large extent standardised; for example in the squares of Bloomsbury and Mayfair, and in the working-class terraces of Manchester and Leeds. Prefabrication was also well established. Since 1830 a number of British factories had specialised in the production of houses for export.

The first attempt to mass-produce houses was made after World War I. In 1917 the British government set up a committee under the chairmanship of John Tudor Walters to consider the post-war reconstruction of working-class housing. The committee reported three weeks before the end of the war in 1918. It noted the deficiencies and recommended a much higher standard of construction, extensive standardisation, and encouragement of the mass production of prefabricated houses. During the next 18 months a total of 88 building systems were approved [198] employing timber, steel, ceramic blocks and precast concrete. They made a useful contribution during the immediate post-war period, but the number of houses prefabricated was relatively small, and their price was no lower than that of traditional construction. After the Depression of 1929 labour was plentiful, building costs fell, and system building was reduced to a very minor role.

After World War II there was an even greater backlog of housing and in Britain a number of demonstration houses were built by 'alternative methods' even before the war ended [198]. The new building systems utilised aluminium (Section 6.2) in addition to the materials previously employed. The timber houses met with some success, but there were not many of these. The metal houses again proved unpopular, and precast concrete emerged as the most successful material for system building, particularly for multi-storey construction [200, 201 and 202]. The main problem in Western Europe was the small number of buildings erected for each system.

System building had been considered in the USSR as part of the Third Five-Year Plan of 1938–42, which was interrupted by the war. The first fully factory-produced concrete buildings were erected in 1949 and, by 1967, more than 3 million square metres (30 million sq ft) of floor space were produced annually for Moscow alone [204].

System building had several advantages for the USSR, because the central control made the number of units for each system much greater; because the residential buildings were predominantly multi-storey, for which system building is better suited; and because the cold winter weather prevented site construction for several months in many parts of the USSR, so that a factory-based method had advantages. However, in spite of these circumstances the cost advantage of prefabrication amounted to only a few per cent, and the main reason for the increasing use of system building in Eastern Europe was its economy in the use of skilled labour.

Factory prefabrication is best suited to timber construction. The units are not as heavy as those of concrete or metal, so that transport of panels to the building site presents fewer problems. Jointing is also easier than for most other materials. Timber is particularly suitable for single-storey houses; prefabricated timber houses have been used extensively in Sweden and more recently in West Germany.

In the USA unsuccessful attempts were made to introduce system building in the European manner, after World Wars I and II, and again in 1969, when the Federal Housing Administration launched Operation Breakthrough [205 and 206] to provide manufactured housing for the underprivileged. The Mobile Home, however, is a uniquely American solution to the same problem.

Travel trailers, called caravans in Britain and Australia, had been manufactured since the 1920s, and in the 1930s as a result of the Depression many people used them for continual residential accommodation. In Europe and Australia this resulted mainly in restrictions on caravan parks; in the USA it led in addition to improvements in the design of trailers.

By 1951 45% of American trailer sales were for primary housing, with toilets and bathrooms commonly installed in these 'mobile homes'. By 1959 mobile homes 3·7 m (12 ft) wide and up to 26 m (85 ft) long were being produced.

This fell a little below the space provided in an American house built by traditional methods, but it was a generous space by Eastern European standards. The mobile home was made by a new industry, which had developed from the trailer factories and was quite separate from the traditional building industry. It was moved in one piece on its own wheels to its destination by a haulier. In this respect it differed from the system-built European house which was assembled on the site from at least three parts brought by special trucks. On arrival at the site, the wheels were removed from the mobile home, it was put on a permanent foundation and generally it was not moved again [205]. By 1972 the cost of a mobile home was less than half that of a traditional house and almost half the new houses in the USA were mobile homes.

6.7. MODULAR COORDINATION AND PREFERRED DIMENSIONS

Mobile homes are perhaps the most successful products of the concept of the *closed system* whereby components are made specifically for one type of dwelling, and used only for that particular type. In the 1960s the concept of the *open system*, which used components from a number of standard catalogues, gained increasing acceptance.

It was originally proposed by Albert Farwell Bemis, an American manufacturer, in the 1920s. In 1936 he published *The Evolving House* [211] in which he proposed the *Cubical Modular Method* 'to improve the inefficient methods of assembly of unrelated materials and reduce the cost of building construction by applying industrial production techniques'. He considered that 4 in (100 mm) provided the largest dimensional increment for minimising problems resulting from stocking and distributing standardised components, while preserving flexibility to meet practical and aesthetic requirements.

After Bemis's death in 1936, his family established the Modular Service Association, which cooperated with the American Standards Association in calling a conference in 1939 to set up a study project with support from the American Institute of Architects and the Producers' Council Inc. [212].

The concept of modular standardisation struck a responsive chord in the European countries faced with a vast rebuilding programme and the European Productivity Agency of the Organisation for European Economic Cooperation set up Project 174 in 1953. This resulted in the acceptance of 4 in and 100 mm (which differed by only 1·6 %) as alternative modules and encouraged further national studies [213, 215 and 216].

In traditional construction lack of fit was overcome by cutting to size materials, such as timber, on the site, adjusting the width of joints, as in brickwork, or providing a cover piece, as in skirting boards. Only the last method is available in prefabricated dry construction. When a closed system building was produced, the manufacturer had full control over the design, the production, and often the erection. In attempting to assemble a building from modular components made by different manufacturers, there needed to be a precise specification of the tolerances of the production process, the distortion during transport and erection, and the relative movement of different parts due to temperature and moisture. The components themselves had to be smaller than an exact multiple of the module by a clearly defined amount to allow them to fit into a modular space.

No standardisation could be achieved if every multiple of 100 mm was an admissible modular size and one effect of modular coordination was a renewed interest in the classical methods of proportioning. Vitruvius [11] had already considered the proportions of the human body (Fig. 6.9), and drawn certain analogies with the desirable proportions of buildings.

Vitruvius also recommended the use of harmonic proportions for the design of buildings. Pythagoras had in the 6th century BC discovered the fixed intervals in the musical scale. In the 4th century BC Plato argued in *Timaeus* that all beauty depends on perfect proportions. A thousand years later, in the 6th century AD, the Christian philosopher Boethius stated in *De Musica* that 'the ear is affected by sounds in quite the same way as the eye is by optical impressions', but the concept seems to have been accepted already in Vitruvius's time, because the ratios primarily recommended by him are 2:1, 5:3 and 3:2 (that is, 2·0, 1·667 and 1·5), all harmonic proportions in the Pythagorean scale.

These ratios were probably used in the buildings of Rome and of the Middle Ages. They became the basis of design in the Renaissance [14, 15 and 207], particularly the ratio 1·667:1.

In the late 19th and the early 20th century many critics claimed that the *golden section* was, in fact, the basis of design of classical and Renaissance buildings and the key to architectural aesthetics. It is a construction, discovered by Eudoxus in the 4th century BC, for dividing a line into two parts so that the shorter part is related to

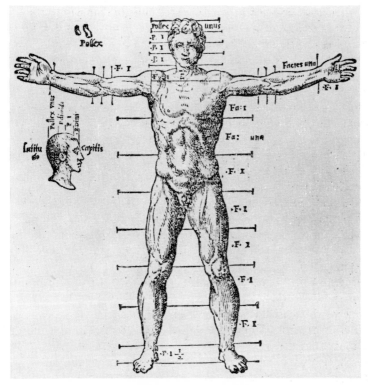

Fig. 6.9. Proportions of the human figure according to Vitruvius [11]. This illustration appeared in Barbaro's Italian translation of Vitruvius's *Ten Books*, published in Venice in 1567.

the longer as the longer is to the whole line; in both cases the ratio is $\frac{1}{2}(1 + [5]^{\frac{1}{2}}) = 1\cdot618$. A Franciscan friar, Luca Pacioli, in 1509 called it *sectio aurea*, golden section. In 1914 Theodore Cook [210] gave the letter φ (the first letter of Pheidias, the Greek sculptor) to the number 1·618.

The golden section has a special association with the Fibonacci series, which is produced by adding each number to the previous number, for example

$$1, 1 + 1 = 2, 2 + 1 = 3, 3 + 2 = 5, 5 + 3 = 8,$$
$$8 + 5 = 13, \text{ and so on.}$$

For the number φ the Fibonacci series gives the same answer as the power series. That is, the series φ, $1 + \varphi$, $1 + 2\varphi$, $2 + 3\varphi$, and so on, gives the same number as the series φ, φ^2, φ^3, φ^4 and so on. This so impressed the astronomer Johann Kepler in the early 17th century that he called the golden section one of the two treasures of geometry.

Claims for the aesthetic qualities of the golden section date only from the middle of the 19th century [208], but by the early 20th century the claim was widely accepted. In fact, the difference between the harmonic ratio of Vitruvius, Alberti and Palladio, 1:1·667, and the golden section 1:1·618, is so small that few people can distinguish between them.

In 1950 Le Corbusier proposed the *Modulor* [209] based on the Fibonacci series of the number φ, together with Bemis's module of 100 mm. He thus produced one series of preferred dimensions

100 mm, 160 mm, 270 mm, 430 mm, 700 mm, 1130 mm, and so on,

and another series of twice that value. The concept of a series of preferred dimensions with increasing increments as the dimensions grew larger was a sound one, but the choice of these complicated numbers based on a geometric construction was unfortunate. The Modulor was widely acclaimed because of Le Corbusier's great reputation, but it was little used in practical design.

In 1943 Ernst Neufert [214] had advocated the division of the module successively by 2, and its multiplication by 3. This gave as preferred numbers

25 mm, 50 mm, 100 mm and 300 mm.

Later 600 mm was added. This series is widely used in both Eastern and Western Europe [216], except that in Eastern Europe 20 mm is substituted for 25 mm.

This rule still leaves more dimensions than are appropriate for a series of preferred dimensions and various client organisations have specified preferred dimensions for their own buildings in order to rationalise the production of components for open-system building.

6.8. THE INDUSTRIALISATION OF BUILDING

Since the beginning of the 19th century the productivity of labour has greatly increased in nearly all industries through the use of mass production techniques. It is sometimes held that the building industry is handicapped by the unpredictability of the weather; but this has not prevented a great reduction in site labour in the building of roads or dams, where machines have largely taken over. Nor is the traditional nature of the industry purely to blame, because it has in fact changed to an extent where building craftsmen trained by 18th-century methods would be of very little use on a modern building site.

If mass production has not made the progress that was hoped for a hundred years ago, a substantial part of the production of buildings has in fact been removed to the factory. The use of cast iron transferred a large part of the work to the foundry and the machine shop (Section 2.1). The time required to erect a modern steel frame is small compared with the time taken up by the fabrication of the steel. The building of timber houses has also changed through the development of the balloon frame in America. Timber is now cut in the saw mill by high speed machinery and assembled by machine-made nails instead of the traditional laborious mortise-and-tenon joints.

The failure to produce so far a generally applicable series of preferred dimensions and the comparative lack of success of system building after two World Wars (Section 6.6) have been disappointing, mainly because the success of standardisation and mass production in industries ranging from the manufacture of clothes to that of automobiles had led to the assumption that similar benefits could be derived from a universal series of preferred dimensions and from the production of system buildings.

Industrialisation has, however, had a considerable success in the organisation of the design and of the construction of buildings. If we assess the relative cost of buildings in terms of the labour expended on them, we find that buildings use far less labour today than they did in the 19th century and, furthermore, that the most industrialised countries have the most efficient building industries. We can do this by determining the number of hours a carpenter or an architect needs to work in order to purchase, say, 200 square metres of residential accommodation of a certain standard. It is found that the American building industry requires fewer hours of labour per square metre than the Russian, and far fewer than that of Ghana. Furthermore, building in the 1970s requires fewer hours of labour than it did in the 1870s. The building costs in developing countries, in spite of the low cost of labour, are not much less than those in developed countries. In comparing the USSR and the USA it is noteworthy that the USSR uses system building and is able to place orders for a large number of identical units, whereas system building is little used by the American building industry; mobile homes are not produced by the building industry.

The explanation is that the building industry in developed countries has undergone a process of industrialisation less spectacular, but far more important than the development of system building or modular coordination. Power tools have greatly reduced labour. In the 19th century it was necessary to cut a square hole into a masonry wall to insert a plug of hardwood in order to attach a conduit; today a bolt is shot into the wall in a fraction of the time and with a fraction of the effort. Bricks, which had to be carried in small batches up a ladder, are now moved by conveyor belt. The concrete mixer, which was the cause of much dirt and manhandling, has been replaced by the ready-mix plant, and so on.

A great deal of standardisation and prefabrication has, in fact, occurred. For example, windows and doors are mostly factory produced to a few standard sizes; building services are partially fabricated in the factory and brought to the building site as sub-assemblies. One reason for the high cost of building in developing countries is the fact that many of these units have to be imported.

Management has greatly improved since the 19th century. Building contractors, particularly in the USA, spend far more time on determining what should be done and far less time on actually doing it. With the aid of the Critical Path Method it is possible to predict with some accuracy when materials need to be delivered, when sub-contractors will be required, when completion of sections of the work may be expected, and what portions of the contract are liable to produce delays unless carefully supervised. Computers have greatly facilitated the evaluation of the data.

The design process has also become industrialised. The design of a large modern office building is far more complex, although less difficult, than that of a Gothic cathedral. The Gothic master builder had no satisfactory method for determining the structural sizes of the cathedral in order to ensure that it did not fall down (Section 1.4); but he did not have to worry unduly about its completion time, he did not have to incorporate services for artificial lighting or air conditioning into the building, or keep accurately within a specified budget.

The modern building has to meet certain standards of thermal comfort, illumination, sound attenuation and audibility. For this purpose it incorporates a variety of building services, many with conflicting requirements and some in conflict with the design of the structure and the facade (Section 5.1). The completion time and the cost must be predicted with accuracy if the project is to be economical. The design thus requires a sophisticated organisation and the aid of data processing facilities.

When the first draft of this book was written in the late 1950s, the conflict between 'modern' and 'traditional' architecture was still acute. Some traditional architects actively disliked modern architecture, and some modern architects wanted to see the eclectic architecture of the late 19th and the early 20th century demolished as quickly as possible and replaced by modern buildings. Today we see a gradual transition between the two schools rather than a sharp break. Many Victorian and Edwardian buildings, once proclaimed as monstrosities, are today considered historical monuments, and few people now regard modern architecture as a temporary aberration.

The problem of reconciling the art of architecture and its technology, however, remains, since most modern buildings are erected for a functional purpose. Gio Ponti [8] has stated the problem:

'Engineering is eclectic; architecture is not. Engineering accepts, experiments with and incorporates, naturally and legitimately, the best available solutions offered by technology and industry, whereby it discharges its whole duty. Engineering creates technical works which are repeatable, multipliable and surpassable. Its works continuously outdo their predecessors. Architecture, being art, is not progressive and tends to create only perpetual unities, expressions which stand by themselves, irrepeatable. It creates works of art that cannot be surpassed, because its expression is an end in itself, and therefore perpetual. It is ridiculous to think of progress in music, painting and poetry. . . . There is a history of painting, music and poetry, but there is no progress in painting, music and poetry.'

The majority of modern buildings compare, as works of art, unfavourably with those surviving from earlier centuries. This is partly because we find it easier to agree on beauty at a distance and partly because architecture, unlike music and literature, is not easily preserved. We occasionally perform a piece of music which is normally relegated to the archives, or take down a rarely read book from the library shelves, only to find that there is a good reason for the oblivion. For the same reason, ugly buildings are more likely to be demolished and thus the surviving old buildings are generally much better than the average of their time. It remains to be seen how many masterpieces will be preserved from the architecture of the past twenty years.

Palladio laid down specific aesthetic rules; this was the reason for the continued popularity of his *Four Books.* It should be possible to write these in the form of a program and produce designs in accordance with Palladio's rules with the graphic output unit of a computer. While one would not expect great art, the result should be comparable to the well-mannered architecture produced by numerous anonymous architects during the Georgian era in England, America and Australia. Unfortunately the computer can offer no help with the aesthetics of modern architecture. We do not know what instructions to give to the computer.

Bibliography

(a) General

Many of the facts may be gathered from a good modern encyclopaedia; however, an old encyclopaedia describes some historical data as recent technological advances. Since many crucial events occurred in the 19th century, the Ninth edition of the *Encyclopaedia Britannica* is particularly helpful, and it is still available in many libraries. It also gives more space to details of classical and medieval history than a modern edition.

1. *Encyclopaedia Britannica*. Ninth Edition. Adam and Charles Black, Edinburgh, 1875–88. 25 volumes.

(b) Modern Books on the History of Architecture

A low-cost book with excellent illustrations, dealing with the whole range from pre-historic to modern buildings:

2. *World Architecture*. Paul Hamlyn, London, 1963. 348 pp.

A standard source of factual information on traditional architecture:

3. Fletcher, Banister (1975). *A History of Architecture by the Comparative Method*, 18th Edition, Athlone Press, London, 1390 pp.

An easily readable paperback on post-classical architecture:

4. Pevsner, N. (1932). *An Outline of European Architecture*, Seventh Edition, Penguin Books, Harmondsworth, 446 pp.

A critical analysis of architecture from 1420 to 1900:

5. Frankl, P. (1968). *Principles of Architectural History*, MIT Press, Cambridge (Mass.), 215 pp.

Two histories of modern architecture:

6. Joedicke, J. (1959). *A History of Modern Architecture*, Architectural Press, London, 243 pp.
7. Pevsner, N. (1968). *The Sources of Modern Architecture and Design*, Thames and Hudson, London, 216 pp.

Three critical analyses of modern architecture:

8. Ponti, G. (1960). *In Praise of Architecture*, F. W. Dodge, New York, 270 pp.
9. Collins, P. (1965). *Changing Ideals of Modern Architecture, 1750–1950*, Faber, London, 309 pp.
10. Boyd, R. (1965). *The Puzzle of Architecture*, Melbourne University Press, Melbourne, 188 pp.

(c) *Reprints of Architectural Classics*

11. Marcus Vitruvius Pollio (Transl. by M. Morgan) (1960). *The Ten Books of Architecture*, Dover Publications, New York, 331 pp. This is a modern translation, based on the original 1st century text, deleting modern additions.
12. Procopius (Greek text with an English translation by H. B. Dewing) (1954). *Buildings*, Heinemann, London, 542 pp.
13. *Filarete's Treatise on Architecture* (edited by J. R. Spencer), Yale University Press, New Haven, 1966, 2 volumes, 339 pp. + facsimile of the manuscript. The first original book on the architecture of the Renaissance.
14. Alberti, Leone Battista (Transl. by J. Leoni) (1955). *Ten Books on Architecture*, Alec Tiranti, London, 256 pp. This is a facsimile on the first English edition of 1755. Alberti reputedly presented the *Ten Books* to Pope Nicholas V in 1452. It was first printed in Latin in 1485, and in Italian in Venice in 1546. Leoni, a Venetian architect, used the Italian version.
15. Palladio, Andrea (1965). *The Four Books of Architecture*, Dover Publications, New York, 110 pp. + 94 plates. This is a facsimile of the English edition published by Isaac Ware in London in 1738. It was first published in Italian in 1570.
16. Wotton, Sir Henry (1968). *The Elements of Architecture*, The University Press of Virginia, Charlottesville, lxxxv + 139 pp. This is a facsimile of the first edition published by John Bill in London in 1624.
17. Eastlake, Charles L. (1970). *A History of the Gothic Revival*, Leicester University Press, Leicester, 209 + 372 pp. Facsimile of the first edition published by Longmans Green and Co. in London in 1872.
18. Ruskin, John (1960). *The Stones of Venice* (Edited and abridged by J. G. Links), Collins, London, 254 pp. This is a modern abridgement of the book first published in 1853.
19. Le Corbusier (Transl. by F. Etchells) (1970). *Towards a New Architecture*, Architectural Press, London, 269 pp. This is a paperback facsimile of the first English edition, published in 1927. The original *Vers une Architecture* was published in Paris in 1923.

Some of the original treatises by Gropius and other pioneers of the modern movement in Germany have been reprinted in two series:

Neue Bauhausbücher, published by Florian Kupferberg in Mainz (German Federal Republic), and
Bauwelt Fundamente, published by Ullstein in West Berlin.

A detailed account of the Bauhaus is given by:

20. Wingler, H. M. (1969). *The Bauhaus*, MIT Press, Cambridge (Mass.), 653 pp.

(d) *Traditional Building Construction*

A paperback on Ancient Egypt, Mesopotamia, India, China, Mexico and Peru:

21. Daniel, G. (1971). *The First Civilizations*, Penguin Books, Harmondsworth, 201 pp.

On Ancient Egypt:

22. Clarke, Somers and Engelbach, R. (1930). *Ancient Egyptian Masonry—The Building Craft*, Oxford University Press, London, 242 pp.
23. Giedion, S. (1964). *The Eternal Present: The Beginnings of Architecture*, Oxford University Press, London, 583 pp.

On Ancient Greece and Rome, including their colonies:

24. Dinsmoor, W. B. (1975). *The Architecture of Ancient Greece*, Norton, New York, 424 pp. (First published in 1944.)
25. Robertson, D. R. (1969). *Greek and Roman Architecture*, First Paperback Edition, Cambridge University Press, London, 407 pp. (First published in 1928.)
26. Allsopp, B. (1965). *A History of Classical Architecture*, Pitman, London, 215 pp.
27. Plommer, H. (1973). *Vitruvius and Later Roman Manuals*, Cambridge University Press, London, 117 pp. This includes the full Latin text and English translation of the treatise *De diversis fabricis architectonicae*, by Cetius Faventinus.
28. Rickman, G. E. (1971). *Roman Granaries and Store Buildings*, Cambridge University Press, London, 349 pp.
29. Merrifield, R. (1969). *Roman London*, Cassell, London, 212 pp.

See also: Refs. 56 to 58, 72 and 86.

On Byzantine and Muslim domes:

30. Baldwin Smith, E. (1971). *The Dome—A Study in the History of Ideas*, Princeton University Press, Princeton, 164 pp.
31. Jantzen, H. (1967). *Die Hagia Sophia des Kaisers Justinian in Konstantinopel* (The Hagia Sophia of the Emperor Justinian in Constantinople), Schauberg, Cologne, 109 pp.
32. Unsal, B. (1970). *Turkish Islamaic Architecture, Seljuk to Ottoman*, Alec Tiranti, London, 116 pp. + 130 plates.
33. Kuran, A. (1968). *The Mosque in Early Ottoman Architecture*, The University of Chicago Press, Chicago, 233 pp.

See also: Refs. 73 and 74.

On Gothic architecture:

34. *The Sketchbook of Villard de Honnecourt* (edited by T. Bowie) (1968). Indiana University Press, Bloomington, 144 pp. A facsimile and translation of one of the very few sketchbooks by a Gothic master mason, probably compiled between 1225 and 1250. Facsimiled from a manuscript in the Bibliothèque Nationale in Paris.
35. Viollet-le-Duc, E. E. (1858–68). *Dictionnaire Raisonné de l'Architecture du XIe au XVIe Siècle*, Librairies-Imprimeries Réunies, Paris, 10 volumes.
36. Scott, Sir G. G. (1879). *Lectures on the Rise and Development of Medieval Architecture Delivered at the Royal Academy*, London, Lecture XV, pp. 212–13.
37. Frankl, P. (1960). *The Gothic*, Princeton University Press, Princeton, 916 pp.

38. Cranage, D. H. S. (1951). *Cathedrals and How They Were Built*, Cambridge University Press, London, 42 pp.
39. Abraham, Pol (1934). *Viollet-le-Duc et le Rationalisme Médiéval*, Fréal, Paris, 116 pp.
40. Fitchen, J. (1961). *The Construction of Gothic Cathedrals*, Oxford University Press, London, 344 pp.

On Renaissance and Baroque domes:
41. Prager, F. and Scaglia, Gustina (1970). *Brunelleschi*, MIT Press, Cambridge (Mass.), 152 pp.
42. Ackerman, J. S. (1970). *The Architecture of Michelangelo*, Penguin Books, London, 373 pp.
43. Guarini, G. (1968). *Architettura Civile*, Edizioni Polifilio, Milan, 471 pp. A reprint of the work published by Guarini in 1683 describing his own domes. It includes geometric constructions of great sophistication for setting out the work.
44. Summerson, J. (1953). *Sir Christopher Wren*, Collins, London, 160 pp.

See also Refs. 71, 80 and 96.

On vernacular construction:
45. Brunskill, R. W. (1970). *Illustrated Handbook of Vernacular Architecture*, Faber, London, 230 pp.
46. Jope, E. M. (Ed.) (1961). *Studies in Building History*, Odhams, London, 287 pp. Fourteen essays on building from Roman Britain to the 17th-century Ireland.
47. Charles, F. W. B. (1967). *Medieval Cruck-Building and its Derivatives*, Society for Medieval Archaelogy, London, 70 pp. + 32 plates.
48. West, Trudy (1971). *The Timber-Frame House in England*, David and Charles, Newton Abbot (Devon), 222 pp.
49. Wight, Jane A. (1972). *Brick Building in England from the Middle Ages to 1550*, John Baker, London, 439 pp.

See also: Refs. 92 to 95.

On construction in Britain:
50. Davey, N. (1964). *Building in Britain*, Evans Brothers, London, 191 pp.
51. Williams, J. A. (1968). *Building and Builders*, Longmans, London, 191 pp.

See also: Refs. 90 and 91.

On construction in North America:
52. Condit, C. W. (1968). *American Building*, University of Chicago Press, Chicago, 329 pp.
53. Randall, F. A. (1949). *History of the Development of Building Construction in Chicago*, University of Illinois Press, Chicago, 385 pp.
54. Condit, C. W. (1964). *The Chicago School of Architecture*, University of Chicago Press, Chicago, 238 pp.
55. Hoffman, Donald (1973). *The Architecture of John Wellborn Root*, Johns Hopkins University Press, Baltimore, 263 pp.

(e) *History of Science and Technology*

Four paperbacks, two dealing with the entire field, and two dealing with important periods in the history of science:

56. Forbes, R. J. and Dijksterhuis, E. J. (1963). *A History of Science and Technology*, Penguin Books, Harmondsworth, 2 volumes, 536 pp.
57. Bernal, J. D. (1965). *Science in History*, Third Edition. Penguin Books, Harmondsworth, 4 volumes, 1328 pp. (4th ed. 1969).
58. Farrington, B. (1963). *Greek Science*, Penguin Books, Harmondsworth, 320 pp.
59. Pledge, H. T. (1966). *Science since 1500*, Second Edition. HM Stationery Office, London, 357 pp.

The following treatises are more specialised:

60. Cohen, M. R. and Drabkin, I. E. (1966). *A Source Book in Greek Science*, Harvard University Press, Cambridge (Mass.), 581 pp. This contains translated passages from Ancient Greek scientific texts.
61. Neugebauer, O. (1957). *The Exact Science in Antiquity*, Brown University Press, Providence (N.I.), 260 pp.
62. Klemm, F. (1959). *A History of Western Technology*, Allen & Unwin, London, 401 pp.
63. Hodges, H. (1970). *Technology in the Ancient World*, Allen Lane, London, 260 pp.
64. Forbes, R. J. (1964). *Studies in Ancient Technology*, E. J. Brill, Leiden, Volume VIII, 288 pp. This volume deals with ancient metallurgy.

(f) *History of Mathematics, Mechanics and Elasticity*

A standard source book on the history of mathematics:

65. Rouse Ball, W. W. (1960). *A Short Account of the History of Mathematics*, Dover Publications, New York, 522 pp. This is a reprint of the Fourth Edition of 1908, and it excludes the 20th century.

An up-to-date and more popular text:

66. Boyer, C. B. (1968). *A History of Mathematics*, Wiley, New York, 717 pp.

The standard source book on the history of the theory of elasticity:

67. Todhunter, I. and Pearson, K. (1960). *A History of the Theory of Elasticity*, Dover Publications, New York, 3 volumes, 2244 pp. A reprint of the 1886–93 edition which excludes the late 19th and the entire 20th century.

The standard book on the wider field of the history of the strength of materials (which includes the theory of elasticity):

68. Timoshenko, S. P. (1953). *History of Strength of Materials*, McGraw-Hill, New York, 452 pp.

A book on mechanics, including some reprints:

69. Truesdell, C. (1968). *Essays in the History of Mechanics*, Springer, New York, 384 pp. This contains articles on mechanics from Leonardo da Vinci to the present time, including some facsimiles.

Two important reprints:

70. Galileo Galilei (1958). *Discorsi e Dimonstrazioni Matematiche Intorno a Due Nuove Scienze Attenenti all Mecanica & i Movimento Locali.* Paolo Boringhieri, Turin, 887 pp. This is a reprint (but not a facsimile) in Italian only of the book originally published by Elzevier in Leiden in 1638. It includes Galileo's theory of bending and his discourse on the strength of materials.

71. Heyman, J. (1972). *Coulomb's Memoir on Statics,* Cambridge University Press, London, 212 pp. This contains a facsimile of the *Essai sur une application des règles de Maximis et Minimis à quelques Problèmes de Statique, relatifs à l'Architecture,* originally published in the *Mémoires de Mathématique & de Physique, présentés à l'Académie Royale des Sciences par divers Savants, & lûs dans ses Assemblées,* Vol. 7 (1773), pp. 343–84, printed in Paris in 1776. It includes an English translation, and a detailed explanatory commentary by Professor Heyman.

Some modern mechanical analyses of traditional structures:

72. Heyman, J. (1972). 'Gothic' construction in Ancient Greece, *J. Soc. Architectural Historians,* **31**, pp. 3–9.

73. Mainstone, R. J. (1965–6). The structure of the church of St Sophia, Istanbul, *Trans. Newcomen Soc.,* **38**, pp. 23–49.

74. Heyman, J. (1967). On shell solution of masonry domes, *Int. J. Solids Struct.,* **3**, pp. 227–41. Includes a solution of St Sophia.

75. Heyman, J. (1966). The stone skeleton, *Int. J. Solids Struct.,* **2**, pp. 249–79. Includes a solution of several Gothic structures.

76. Heyman, J. (1967). Spires and fan vaults, *Int. J. Solids Struct.,* **3**, pp. 243–57.

77. Heyman, J. (1967–8). Beauvais Cathedral, *Trans. Newcomen Soc.,* **40**, pp. 15–35.

78. Heyman, J. (1969). The safety of masonry arches, *Int. J. Mech. Sci.,* **11**, pp. 363–85.

79. Heyman, J. *et al.* (1972). Two masonry bridges: Clare College Bridge and Telford's Bridge at Over, *Proc. Inst. Civ. Eng.,* **52**, pp. 305–30.

80. Mainstone, R. J. (1969–70). Brunelleschi's dome S. Maria del Fiore and some related structures, *Trans. Newcomen Soc.,* **42**, pp. 107–26.

81. Heyman, J. (1967). Westminster Hall roof, *Proc. Inst. Civ. Eng.,* **37**, pp. 137–62. This is an analysis of the famous medieval timber roof, completed in 1402.

82. Castigliano, A. (1966). *The Theory of Equilibrium of Elastic Systems and its Application,* Dover Publications, New York, 360 pp. This is a facsimile of the English translation by E. S. Andrews originally published in 1919. The translation was made from the French version published in Turin in 1879.

83. Cross, Hardy (1963). *Selected Papers in Arches, Continuous Frames, Frames and Conduits,* University of Illinois Press, Urbana, 265 pp.

The original paper on the slope-deflection method:

84. Wilson, W. M. and Maney, G. A. 'Wind stresses in Office Buildings,' Bulletin No. 80. Engineering Experiment Station, University of Illinois, Urbana, 1915.

(g) *History of Engineering*

A bibliography:
85. Ferguson, E. S. (1968). *Bibliography of the History of Technology*, MIT Press, Cambridge (Mass.), 347 pp.

Four general books:
86. Sprague de Camp, L. (1960). *The Ancient Engineers*, Doubleday, New York, 408 pp. Covers the subject from prehistoric times up to and including the Renaissance.
87. Hammond, Rolt (1964). *The Forth Bridge and its Builders*, Eyre and Spottiswoode, London, 226 pp.
88. Pannell, J. P. M. (1964). *An Illustrated History of Civil Engineering*, Thames and Hudson, London, 376 pp. Primarily concerned with public works in Britain.
89. Armytage, W. H. G. (1970). *A Social History of Engineering*, Third Edition. Faber, London, 379 pp. Deals mainly with heavy industry in Britain.

On the industrial archaeology (*i.e.* the remains of old engineering works) of Britain:
90. Raistrick, A. (1972). *Industrial Archaeology*, Eyre Methuen, London, 314 pp.
91. Wilson, A. (1967). *London's Industrial Heritage*, David and Charles, Newton Abbot (Devon), 160 pp.

On ancient machines:
92. Burstall, A. F. (1968). *Simple Working Models of Historic Machines, Easily Made by the Reader*, Arnold, London, 79 pp. Models of machines from Ancient China, the Hellenistic period of Egypt, and medieval Europe.
93. Keller, A. G. (1964). *A Theatre of Machines*, Chapman and Hall, London, 155 pp. Plates reproduced from books printed between 1570 and 1630.
94. Taccola, Mariano di Jacopo detto il (1969). *Liber Tertius de Ingeneis ac Edifitiis non Usitatis*, Edizioni Il Polifolio, Milan, 156 pp. Facsimile of a 15th-century manuscript, with printed version of the handwritten Latin text.
95. Jensen, M. (1969). *Civil Engineering around 1700,* Danish Technical Press, Copenhagen, 207 pp. Machines used around 1700.

General William Barclay Parsons's treatise has recently been reprinted. It contains a detailed account of the contribution of Leonardo da Vinci, illustrations of machines used in the Renaissance, early attempts at analysis of several bridges, including the Rialto Bridge in Venice and the Pont Neuf in Paris, and of the Florence Duomo and St Peter's in Rome (the last incomplete):
96. Parsons, W. B. (1967). *Engineers and Engineering in the Renaissance*, MIT Press, Cambridge (Mass.), 661 pp. The book was originally published, posthumously, in 1939 by Williams and Wilkins.

The two original volumes by Samuel Smiles are still in many libraries, but it is a very wordy treatise. An abridged edition is now available:
97. *Lives of the Engineers, Selections from Samuel Smiles* (edited by T. P. Hughes), MIT Press, Cambridge (Mass.), 1966, 447 pp.

Modern books covering 19th-century British civil engineering:
98. Boucher, C. T. (1963). *John Rennie 1761–1821*, Manchester University Press, Manchester, 148 pp.
99. Thomas, J. (1972). *The Tay Bridge Disaster*, David and Charles, Newton Abbot (Devon), 208 pp.
100. Rolt, L. T. C. (1970). *Victorian Engineering*, Allen Lane, London, 300 pp.

The Transactions of the Newcomen Society are a fruitful source of information, particularly on Britain.

(h) Engineering Structures

We have dealt with construction and with the theory of traditional structures in previous sections and also with the history of mechanics and of the theory of elasticity.

An art historian's point of view:
101. Giedion, S. (1967). *Space, Time and Architecture*, Fifth Edition, Harvard University Press, Cambridge (Mass.), 897 pp.

On the relation between structure and form:
102. Mainstone, Rowland J. (1975). *Developments in Structural Form*, Allen Lane, London, 350 pp.

Two surveys from an engineer's point of view:
103. Straub, H. (1952). *A History of Civil Engineering*, Leonard Hill, London, 258 pp.
104. Lanchester, F. W. (1939). *Span*, Butterly and Wood, Manchester, 100 pp. An invitation lecture delivered to the Manchester Association of Engineers by Dr F. W. Lanchester, better known for his pioneering work on the design of automobiles. It shows an early insight into the problem of span and contains the first proposals for the design of pneumatic structures with a span of the order of 420 m (1400 ft).

(i) Iron and Steel Structures

105. Hamilton, S. B. (1957–9). The structural use of iron in antiquity, *Trans. Newcomen Soc.*, **31**, pp. 29–47.
106. Schubert, H. R. (1957). *History of the British Iron and Steel Industry from 450 BC to AD 1775*, Routledge and Kegan Paul, London, 305 pp.
107. Johnson, H. R. and Skempton, W. (1955–7). William Strutt's cotton mills, *Trans. Newcomen Soc.*, **30**, pp. 179–205.
108. Skempton, A. W. and Johnson, H. R. (March 1962). The first iron frames, *Architectural Review*, **114**, pp. 175–86.
109. Tredgold, T. (1824). *Practical Essay on the Strength of Cast Iron*, J. Taylor, London, 305 pp. A standard textbook in the early 19th century, still available in many libraries.
110. Wittek, K. H. (1964). *Die Entwicklung des Stahlhochbaus* (The development of steel structures), VDI Verlag, Dusseldorf, 122 pp.
111. Robertson, A. 'The Strength of Struts', Selected Engineering Paper No. 28, Institution of Civil Engineers, London, 1925, 55 pp.

112. Baker, J. F. (1954 and 1956). *The Steel Skeleton*, Cambridge University Press, London, 2 volumes 206 + 408 pp. This gives the historical background to the plastic design of steel structures.

See also: Refs. 52 to 54.

The *Transactions of the Newcomen Society* contain many papers on early structures in iron and steel.

(j) Concrete Structures

On Ancient Roman concrete:

113. Blake, M. E. (1947). *Ancient Roman Construction in Italy from the Prehistoric Period to August*, Carnegie Inst. Pub. 570, Washington, 421 pp. + 57 plates.
114. Blake, M. E. (1959). *Roman Construction in Italy from Tiberius through to the Flavians*. Carnegie Inst., Pub. 616, Washington, 195 pp. + 31 plates.
115. Blake, M. E. (1973). *Roman Construction in Italy from Nerva through to the Antonines*, American Philosophical Society, Memoir Volume 96, Philadelphia, 304 pp. + 36 plates.
116. Davey, N. (1974). Roman concrete and mortar, *Structural Engineer*, **52**, pp. 193–95.

See also: Refs. 11, 27 and 86.

On ancient and 19th-century concrete structures:

117. Haegermann, G., Huberti, G. and Moll, H. (1964). *Vom Caementum zum Spannbeton* (From caementum to prestressed concrete), Bauverlag, Wiesbaden, 2 volumes, 491 pp.
118. Cowan, H. J. (1975). *The Design of Reinforced Concrete*, Chapter 2. The History of Reinforced Concrete, Sydney University Press, Sydney, pp. 10–17.
119. Draffin, J. O. 'A Brief History of Lime, Cement, Concrete and Reinforced Concrete,' University of Illinois Engineering Experiment Station, Reprint No. 27, 1943, 47 pp.
120. Davis, A. C. (1924). *A Hundred Years of Portland Cement*, Concrete Publications, London, 277 pp.
121. Cassie, W. F. (1955). Early reinforced concrete in Newcastle upon Tyne, *Structural Engineer*, **33**, pp. 134–7.
122. Hamilton, S. B. 'A note on the history of reinforced concrete in buildings,' National Building Studies, Special Report No. 24, HM Stationery Office, London, 1956, 30 pp.
123. Fiftieth Anniversary Number (1956). *Concrete and Constructional Engineering*, **51**, pp. 1–262. Ordinary issues of the journal, and its successor *Concrete*, also contain articles of historical interest.
124. Anniversary issue (1954). *J. American Concrete Institute*, **35**, pp. 409–524. Other issues of this journal also contain articles of historical interest.

Smeaton's own description of his re-discovery of waterproof cement:

125. Smeaton, John (1813). *The Narrative of the Building of the Eddystone Lighthouse with Stone*, Longman, Hurst, Rees, Orme and Brown, London, 198 pp.

Some early books on reinforced concrete are still available in many libraries:

126. Berger, C. and Guillerme, V. (1902). *La Construction en Ciment Armé*, Ch. Dunod, Paris, 2 volumes, 886 pp. + 69 plates.
127. Marsh, C. F. (1904). *Reinforced Concrete*, Constable, London, 545 pp.
128. Mörsch, E. (1909). *Concrete Steel Construction* (English translation of *Der Eisenbetonbau*), Engineering News Publishing Co., New York, 368 pp.
129. *Preliminary and Second Reports of the Committee on Reinforced Concrete*, Institution of Civil Engineers, London, 1913, 2 volumes, 262 + 187 pp.
130. Emperger, F. (Ed.) (1921). *Handbuch für Stahlbetonbau* (Handbook of reinforced concrete), Third Edition, Volume 1. The elements of the historical development of reinforced concrete, experiments and theory (in German). W. Ernst, Berlin, 800 pp.

Original contributions to the design of reinforced concrete slabs:

131. Marcus, H. (1924). *Die Theorie elastischer Gewebe und ihre Anwendung auf die Berechnung biegsamer Platten* (The theory of elastic networks and its application to the flexural design of thick plates), Julius Springer, Berlin.
132. Eddy, Henry T. and Turner, C. A. P. (1919). *Concrete–Steel Construction, Part I—Buildings*, Second Edition. Privately published, Minneapolis, 477 pp.
133. Westergaard, H. M. and Slater, W. A. (1921). Moments and stresses in slabs, *Proc. American Concrete Institute*, 17, pp. 415–525.
134. Di Stasio, J. (1941). Flat plate rigid frame design of low cost housing projects in Newark and Atlantic City, N.J., *Proc. American Concrete Institute*, 37, pp. 309–24.

Some books on the form of modern concrete structures:

135. Raafat, A. A. (1858). *Reinforced Concrete in Architecture*, Reinhold, New York, 240 pp.
136. Collins, P. (1959). *Concrete, the Vision of a New Architecture*, Faber, London, 307 pp.
137. Bill, M. (1969). *Robert Maillart*, Pall Mall Press, London, 184 pp.
138. Nervi, P. L. (Transl. by M. and G. Salvadori) (1956). *Structures*, Dodge, New York, 118 pp.
139. *The Structures of Eduardo Torroja—An Autobiography of Engineering Accomplishment*, Dodge, New York, 1858. 198 pp.
140. Boaga, B. and Boni, B. (1965). *The Concrete Architecture of Ricardo Morandi*, Tiranti, London, 234 pp.
141. *Nicolas Esquillan—Cinquante Ans à l'Avant-Garde du Génie Civil* (Esquillan —50 years in the forefront of civil engineering), Syndicat National du Béton Armé et des Techniques Industrialisées, Paris, 1974. 118 pp.

On prestressed concrete:

142. *Conference on Prestressed Concrete*. Institution of Civil Engineers, London, 1949. 132 pp. This gives an early English view of the problem, and includes an historical sketch.
143. Möll, H. (1954). *Spannbeton* (Prestressed concrete), Berliner Union, Stuttgart, 272 pp. An account of patent systems registered in Germany by the President of the German Patent Court.

The international conferences organised by the Fédération Internationale de la Précontrainte, London, contain some papers of historical interest.

On ultimate strength design:

144. Report of the ASCE–ACI Joint Committee on Ultimate Strength Design. *Proc. American Soc. Civ. Eng.*, **81** (1955), Paper 809, 68 pp. This report led to the adoption of ultimate strength design; it includes an historical survey.
145. Johansen, K. W. (1962). *Yield-Line Theory*, Cement and Concrete Association, London, 181 pp. This is the English translation of the original book on the yield-line theory, published in Denmark in 1943.

(k) Fire Protection

146. Hamilton, S. B. (1958). *A Short History of the Structural Fire Protection of Building*, HM Stationery Office, London, 73 pp.
147. Lie, T. T. (1972). *Fire and Buildings*, Applied Science Publishers, London, 276 pp.
148. Roetter, C. (1962). *Fire is their Enemy*, Angus and Robertson, Sydney, 184 pp.
149. Himmelwright, A. L. A. (1907). *The San Francisco Earthquake and Fire*, 1906, The Roebling Construction Company, New York.
150. *Proceedings of the Symposium on the Fire Protection of High Rise Buildings*, Chicago Committee on High Rise Buildings and Illinois Institute of Technology, Chicago, 1972. 303 pp.

(l) Shell Structures

Early reinforced concrete shells are described in:

151. von Klass, G. (1955). *Weit spannt sich der Bogen* (Great is the span of the arch), Dyckerhoff and Widmann, Munich, 234 pp. This was published on the occasion of its centenary by the firm which built the first reinforced concrete shells.

See also: Refs. 135, 137 and 139.

On shell form:

152. Joedicke, J. (1962). *Schalenbau* (Shell construction), Karl Kramer Verlag, Stuttgart, 304 pp.
153. Faber, C. (1963). *Candela: Shell Builder*, Reinhold, New York, 240 pp.

See also: Refs. 138, 139 and 141.

The membrane theory by Dischinger, originally published in *Der Bauingenieur* in 1928, is reproduced in:

154. Pflüger, A. (1961). *Elementary Statics of Shells*, Dodge, New York, 122 pp.

The general theory is discussed in many books, for example:

155. Haas, A. M. (1962 and 1967). *Thin Concrete Shells*, Wiley, New York, 2 volumes, 129 + 242 pp.

156. Wlassow, W. S. (Vlasov, V. Z.) (1958). *Allgemeine Schalentheorie und ihre Anwendung auf die Technik*, Akademie Verlag, (East) Berlin, 661 pp. There is no English translation of this standard Russian text at present.

The original paper on the design of folded-plate structures by moment distribution:

157. Winter, G. and Pei, M. (1947). Hipped-plate construction, *Proc. American Concrete Institute*, **43**, pp. 505–31.

The proceedings of international conferences organised by the International Association for Shell Structures, Madrid, and its *Bulletin* contain papers of historical interest.

(*m*) *Space Frames*

Schwedler's original paper on triangulated domes:

158. Schwedler, J. W. A. (1866). Theorie der Kuppelflächen (Theory of dome surfaces), *Zeitschrift für Bauwesen* (Berlin), p. 7.
159. Wachsmann, K. (1961). *The Turning Point in Building*, Reinhold, New York, 239 pp. Some early concepts by one of the original staff members of the Bauhaus.
160. Marks, R. W. (1960). *The Dymaxion World of Buckminster Fuller*, Reinhold, New York, 232 pp.
161. Makowski, Z. S. (1965). *Steel Space Structures*, Michael Joseph, London, 214 pp.
162. *Proceedings of the First International Conference on Space Structures*, Blackwell, Oxford, 1967, 1233 pp.

(*n*) *Suspension Structures and Pneumatic Structures*

163. *Hanging Roofs*, North-Holland, Amsterdam, 1963. 335 pp. This account of the Paris Colloquium held in 1962 by the International Association for Shell Structures deals with early work.
164. *Tension Structures and Space Frames*, Architectural Institute of Japan, Tokyo, 1972. 1042 pp. This recent symposium was also organised by the IASS.
165. Otto, F. (1967). *Tensile Structures*, MIT Press, Cambridge (Mass.), Volume 1. Pneumatic Structures. 320 pp. Volume 2. Cables, Nets and Membranes. 171 pp.
166. Dent, R. N. (1971). *Principles of Pneumatic Architecture*, Architectural Press, London, 236 pp.

See also: Ref. 104.

(*o*) *Loads*

167. Dunham, J. W. *et al.* 'Live Loads on Floors in Buildings,' National Bureau of Standards, Building Materials and Structures Report 133, Superintendent of Documents, Washington 1952, 27 pp. This includes an account of two important earlier studies, one carried out by the National Bureau of Standards in 1924, and the other carried out by C. M. White in Britain, and included in the First Report of the Steel Structures Research Committee in 1931.

168. Mitchell, G. R. 'Loadings on Buildings—A Review Paper,' Building Research Station Current Paper 50–69, Ministry of Public Buildings and Works, London, 1969, 9 pp. This reviews recent British work.
169. Hatt, W. K. (1907). Notes on the effect of time element in loading reinforced concrete beams, *Proc. American Soc. Testing Materials*, **7**, pp. 421–23. An early observation of the phenomenon later called creep.
170. Schriever, W. R. and Ostvanov, V. A. Snow loads—preparation of standards for snow loads on roofs in various countries, with particular reference to the USSR and Canada, in 'On Methods of Load Calculation,' CIB Report No. 9. International Council for Building Research Studies and Documentation. Rotterdam, 1967, pp. 13–33.
171. McCrea, J. D. 'Wind Action on Structures,' Bibliography No. 5, Division of Building Research, Ottawa, 1952. 6 pp. This is a comprehensive bibliography of early work, going back to 1759.
172. *Proceedings of the Third International Conference on Wind Effects on Buildings and Structures*. Saikon, Tokyo, 1972. 1267 pp. This is the latest conference. Proceedings of the two previous conferences were published by HM Stationery Office, in London in 1965, and by the University of Toronto Press in 1968.
173. Architectural Institute of Japan (1970). *Design Essentials in Earthquake Resistant Buildings*, Elsevier, Amsterdam, 295 pp.
174. Newmark, J. M. and Rosenblueth, E. (1971). *Fundamental of Earthquake Engineering*, Prentice-Hall, Englewood Cliffs (N.J.), 640 pp.

Reports of the major earthquakes are contained in the *Bulletin of the Seismological Society of America*, and in the *Proceedings of the World Conferences on Earthquake Engineering*, held in California in 1956, in Japan in 1960, in New Zealand in 1965 and in Chile in 1969. Reports on damage done in specific earthquakes have also been issued by the US Department of Commerce and by the American Iron and Steel Institute.

175. Griffiths, H., Pugsley, Sir A. and Saunders, Sir O. (1968). *Report of the Enquiry into the Collapse of Flats at Ronan Point, Canning Town*, HM Stationery Office, London, 71 pp.

The gas explosion examined in this report started discussion in many countries of the problems created by internal explosions. These are considered by Working Commission W23a of the International Council for Building Research in:

176. Lewicki, B. and Olesen, S. O. (1974). Limiting the possibility of progressive collapse, *Building Research and Practice*, **2**, pp. 10–13.
177. Rhodes, Peter S. (1974). The structural assessment of buildings subjected to bomb damage, *Structural Engineer*, **52**, pp. 329–39.
178. Empire State Building intact after bomber hits 79th floor, *Engineering News Record*, **135** (1935), pp. 129–30.

(p) Tall Buildings

Both the history and the current practice are covered in great detail in the proceedings of the international conference held at Lehigh University in 1972:

179. *Planning and Design of Tall Buildings*, American Society of Civil Engineers, New York, 1973, 5 volumes, 5138 pp.

(q) Model Analysis of Structures

Both the history and the current practice are discussed in:

180. Cowan, H. J. *et al*. (1968). *Models in Architecture*, Elsevier, London, 228 pp.

The first paper on indirect model analysis:

181. Beggs, G. E. (1922). The accurate mechanical solution of statically indeterminate structures by the use of paper models and special gauges, *J. American Concrete Institute*, **18**, pp. 58–78.

Many important direct model tests of buildings are described by:

182. Fumagalli, E. (1973). *Statical and Geomechanical Models*, Springer, Vienna, 182 pp.

(r) Analogue Computers for Structural Design

183. Bush, Vannevar (1934). Structural analysis by electric circuit analogues, *J. Franklin Institute*, **217**, p. 289.
184. Ryder, Frederick L. (Dec. 1953). Electrical analogs for statically loaded structures, *Proc. American Soc. Civ. Eng.*, **79**, Separate No. 376, 24 pp.

(s) Digital Computers for Structural Design

A popular history of computers:

185. Eames, Charles and Eames, Ray (1973). *A Computer Perspective*, Harvard University Press, Cambridge, 174 pp.

The first paper on the computer analysis of an architectural structure:

186. Livesley, R. K. (1953). Analysis of rigid frames by an electronic digital computer, *Engineering*, **176**, pp. 230 and 277.

Early progress can be gauged from the proceedings of the First and Second Conferences on Electronic Computation, held by the American Society of Civil Engineers in 1958 and 1960. There is now a vast and growing literature, including many books, for example:

187. Harrison, H. B. (1973). *Computer Methods in Structural Analysis*, Prentice-Hall, Englewood Cliffs (N.J.), 337 pp.

(t) Building Research

The history of the oldest building research organisation was on the occasion of its 50th anniversary reviewed by a former director:

188. Lea, F. M. (1971). *Science and Building—A History of the Building Research Station*. HM Stationery Office, London, 203 pp.

Most building research organisations issue annual reports. Their addresses are listed in Appendix C.2 of the *Dictionary of Architectural Science*, Applied Science, London, 1973, pp. 236–8.

(*u*) *Building Materials*

The subjects discussed under m, n, o, p, q, r, s and t deal with recent innovations: a twenty-year-old paper on the computer analysis of architectural structures might be considered as being of 'historical' interest. By contrast, evidence on the use of building materials may be gathered on pre-historic sites, from classical buildings, and from writings. Attention is drawn particularly to Refs. 11, 14, 15, 27, 45 to 47, 64, 86, 88, 90, 91, 105, 106, 109 and 113 to 125. The entire subject is covered by:

189. Davey, N. (1961). *A History of Building Materials*, Phoenix House, London, 260 pp.

Books on materials not previously mentioned, which include a brief history of their use in building:

190. Brimelow, E. I. (1957). *Aluminium in Buildings*, Macdonald, London, 378 pp.
191. McGrath, R. *et al.* (1961). *Glass in Architecture and Decoration*, Architectural Press, London, 712 pp.
192. Harden, D. B. (1961). 'Domestic window glass—Roman, Saxon, Medieval', in *Studies in Building History* (Edited by E. M. Jope), Odhams, London, pp. 39–63.
193. Couzens, E. G. and Yarsley, V. E. (1968). *Plastics*, Penguin Books, Harmondsworth, 386 pp.
194. Hurst, A. E. (1963). *Painting and Decorating*, Griffin, London, 482 pp.

(*v*) *Industrialised Building*

There are several books on the construction of the Crystal Palace and other 19th-century prefabricated iron structures, for example:

195. Hobhouse, C. (1937). *1851 and the Crystal Palace*, Murray, London, 181 pp.
196. Beaver, P. (1970). *The Crystal Palace*, Evelyn, London, 151 pp.

See also: Refs. 17 and 159.

Nineteenth-century prefabricated concrete structures are described by:

197. Petersen, J. L. (1954). History and development of precast concrete in the United States, *J. American Concrete Institute*, **35**, pp. 477–500.

The history of prefabricated housing in Britain, particularly in the early 20th century, is described by:

198. White, R. B. 'Prefabrication—A History of its Development in Great Britain', National Building Studies, Special Report No. 36, HM Stationery Office, London, 1965, 354 pp.

The proceedings of the Third International Building Research Congress, held under CIB auspices in Copenhagen in 1965, contain a survey of the position throughout the world at the time:

199. *Towards Industrialised Building*, Elsevier, Amsterdam, 1966, 493 pp.

The position in Western Europe was considered at two conferences:

200. *Housing from the Factory*, Cement and Concrete Association, London, 1962, 151 pp.
201. *Industrialised Building and the Structural Engineer*, Institution of Structural Engineers, London, 1966, 332 pp.

On Central Europe:

202. Koncz, T. *Manual of Precast Concrete Construction*, Bauverlag, Wiesbaden, 1968–70, 3 volumes, 1099 pp.

On Eastern Europe:

203. Sebestyén, G. (1965). *Large Panel Buildings*, Publishing House of the Hungarian Academy of Sciences, Budapest, 401 pp.
204. Promyslov, V. F. (1967). *Moscow in Construction*, MIR Publishers, Moscow, 365 pp.

On America:

205. *Industrialised Building Systems for Housing*, MIT Press, Cambridge (Mass.), 1971, 260 pp. A compendium based on an MIT Special Summer Session.
206. 'Systems Building', Proceedings of a Conference held at Gaithersburg, Maryland, 24–26 February, 1972, sponsored by the American Society of Civil Engineers and the National Science Foundation, 343 pp. This volume differs from the others in emphasising the benefits to be derived from management systems as well as construction systems.

(w) Theories of Proportion and Modular Coordination

Theories of proportion are reviewed by:

207. Wittkower, R. (1962). *Architectural Principles in the Age of Humanism*, Third Edition, Alec Tiranti, London, 173 pp. + 48 plates.
208. Schofield, P. H. (1958). *The Theory of Proportion in Architecture*, Cambridge University Press, London, 156 pp.

The modern revival by Le Corbusier:

209. Le Corbusier (Transl. by P. de Francia and A. Bostock) (1954). *The Modulor*, Faber, London, 243 pp. Originally published in French in 1950.

The use of the ratio φ (Golden Section) in theories of proportion is largely due to Sir Theodore Cook:

210. Cook, Theodore Andrea (1914). *The Curves of Life*, Constable, London, 479 pp.

The original treatise on modular coordination:

211. Bemis, A. F. (1936). *The Evolving House*, Volume 3: Rational Design Technology Press, Cambridge (Mass.), 625 pp.

This led to the formation of the Modular Building Standards Association, whose work is reviewed in:

212. *Modular Practice*, Wiley, New York, 1962, 198 pp.

The British work is reviewed in:

213. *The Co-ordination of Dimensions for Building*, Royal Institute of British Architects, London, 1965, 87 pp.

Three statements of Continental practice:

214. Neufert, E. (1965). *Bauordnungslehre* (Handbook for rational building), Bauverlag, Wiesbaden, 336 pp.
215. Bussat, P. (1963). *La Coordination Modulaire dans le Bâtiment*, Kramer, Stuttgart, 80 pp.
216. Nissen, H. (Transl. by P. Katborg) (1972). *Industrialised Building and Modular Design*, Cement and Concrete Association, London, 443 pp. This is translated from the standard Danish text originally published in 1966.

(*x*) *Thermal Properties of Buildings*

The Ancient Roman concepts on the effect of climate on design are given in Vitruvius [11] Book VI.

The medieval view of climatology is briefly described by:

217. Thorndike, L. (1949). *The Sphere of Sacrobosco and its Commentators*, University of Chicago Press, Chicago, p. 129.

The first paper on sun-machines:

218. Dufton, A. F. and Beckett, H. E. (1932). The heliodon—an instrument for demonstrating the apparent motion of the sun, *J. Scientific Instruments*, **9**, pp. 251–6.

Traditional and modern methods of sun control are explained by:

219. Olgyay, V. (1963). *Design with Climate*, Princeton University Press, Princeton, 190 pp.

Research on thermal comfort in the 19th and early 20th century is described by:

220. Bedford, T. (1964). *Basic Principles of Ventilation and Heating*, Second Edition. H. K. Lewis, London, 438 pp.

An early physiological observation:

221. Blagden, D. (1775). Experiments and observations in a heated room, *Phil. Trans. Roy. Soc. London*, **65**, p. 111.

The problems of acclimatisation to the tropics are discussed by:

222. Markham, S. F. (1947). *Climate and the Energy of Nations*, Oxford University Press, London, 240 pp.

An architect's view of the problems set by hot climate:

223. Fry, Maxwell and Drew, Jane (1964). *Tropical Architecture*, Batsford, London, 264 pp.

The concept of effective temperature:

224. Houghten, F. C. and Yaglou, C. P. (1923). Determination of the comfort zone, *Trans. Amer. Soc. Heating and Ventilating Engineers*, **29**, p. 361.

The concept of equivalent temperature:

225. Dufton, A. F. 'The Equivalent Temperature of a Room and its Measurement,' Building Research Technical Paper No. 13, HM Stationery Office, London, 1932, 8 pp.

The comfort criterion most widely accepted at the time of writing is due to Fanger:

226. Fanger, P. O. (1970). *Thermal Comfort*, Danish Technical Press, Copenhagen, 244 pp.

(y) Heating, Ventilating and Air Conditioning

A history of medieval heating is given by:

227. Billington, N. (1959). A historical review of the art of heating and ventilating, *Architectural Science Review*, **2**, pp. 118–30.

Professor Banham views modern building services in their historical context:

228. Banham, R. (1969). *The Architecture of the Well-tempered Environment*, Architectural Press, London, 295 pp.

A statement of current practice is given in the manual authored by the company which pioneered air conditioning.

229. Carrier Air Conditioning Company, *Handbook of Air Conditioning Design*, McGraw-Hill, New York, 1965, 871 pp.

Carrier's biography:

230. Ingels, Margaret (1952). *Willis Haviland Carrier, Father of Air Conditioning*. Country Life Press, Garden City (New York), 176 pp.

On the architectural problems of solar water heaters:

231. Thau, A. (1973). Architectural and town planning aspects of domestic solar water heaters, *Architectural Science Review*, **16**, pp. 89–104.

Articles of historical interest may be found in the journals of the American Society of Heating, Refrigeration and Air Conditioning Engineers, and the (British) Institution of Heating and Ventilating Engineers.

(z) Lighting

232. O'Dea, W. T. (1958). *A Short History of Lighting*, HM Stationery Office, London, 40 pp.

233. Walsh, J. W. T. (1961). *The Science of Daylight*, Macdonald, London, 285 pp. This includes an historical survey.

234. Hopkinson, R. G. and Collins, J. B. (1970). *The Ergonomics of Lighting*, Macdonald, London, 272 pp.

235. Moon, P. and Spencer, D. E. (Dec. 1942). Illumination from a non-uniform sky, *Illuminating Engineering*, **37**, pp. 707–26.
236. Harris, Moses (1963). *The Natural System of Colours*, Whitney Library of Design, New York. A facsimile of an early work in colour, published in 1766.

(aa) Acoustics

The Ancient Roman concepts on acoustics are given in Vitruvius [11], Book V.

A modern view of Greek and Roman acoustics is given by:

237. Canac, F. (1967). *L'Acoustique des Théâtres Antiques—ses Enseignements* (The acoustics of ancient theatres—their lessons), Centre National de la Recherche Scientifique, Paris, 181 pp.

A brief account of the acoustics of the Middle Ages and the Renaissance is given by:

238. Richardson, E. G. (1945). *Acoustics for Architects*, Arnold, London, pp. 19–26.
239. Richardson, E. G. (1954). Acoustics in modern life, *Science Progress*, **42**, pp. 232–9.

A brief account of the evolution of musical instruments is given by:

240. Backus, J. (1970). *The Acoustical Foundations of Music*, Murray, London, 312 pp.

Some of the papers of Professor Sabine have been reprinted:

241. Sabine, W. C. (1964). *Collected Papers on Acoustics*, Dover Publications, New York, 279 pp.

Some of the mythology of concert hall acoustics is discussed by:

242. Beranek, L. L. (1962). *Music, Acoustics and Architecture*, Wiley, New York, 586 pp.

Noise control is too recent a subject to have a substantial history. However, a good account of the development of the problem is given in:

243. Beranek, Leo L. (Ed.) (1960). *Noise Reduction*, McGraw-Hill, New York, 752 pp.
244. Committee on the Problem of Noise, *Noise—Final Report*, HM Stationery Office, London, 1963, 235 pp.

(bb) Vertical Transportation

The effect of the invention of the passenger lift on the development of tall buildings is described by Randall [53] and by Condit [54].

The current practice is given by:

245. Adler, R. R. (1970). *Vertical Transportation for Buildings*, Elsevier, New York, 228 pp.

(cc) Water Supply and Waste Disposal

Ancient Roman aqueducts are described by:

246. Winslow, W. M. (1963). *A Libation to the Gods*, Hodder and Stoughton, London, 191 pp.

Ancient Roman sewerage systems are described by:

247. Carcopino, J. (1956). *Daily Life in Ancient Rome*, Penguin Books, Harmondsworth, p. 49.
248. Fraser, W. M. (1950). *A History of English Public Health*, 1834–1839, Ballière, Tindall and Cox, London, 498 pp.
249. Wright, Lawrence (1960). *Clean and Decent*, Routledge and Kegan Paul, London, 282 pp.

See also: Ref. 88.

The Chadwick Report has recently been reprinted in abridged form:

250. Chadwick, Edwin (1965). *Report on the Sanitary Condition of the Labouring Population of Great Britain*, originally published in 1842. Abridged and edited by W. M. Flinn. Edinburgh University Press, Edinburgh, 443 pp.

A short history of American plumbing:

251. Nielsen, L. S. (1963). *Standard Plumbing Engineering Design*, McGraw-Hill, New York, 312 pp.

The building of the Croton Aqueduct, New York, the first to be built in the 19th century, is described by:

252. Fitzsimons, N. (Ed.) (1971). *The Reminiscences of John B. Jervis—Engineer of Old Croton*, Syracuse University Press, Syracuse, (N.Y.), 196 pp.

Abbreviations

a.c.	alternating current	ksi	kilopounds per square inch
AD	anno domini	lb	pound
BC	before Christ	m	metre
C	Celsius	min	minute
d.c.	direct current	mm	millimetre
F	Fahrenheit	MPa	megapascal
ft	foot	mph	miles per hour
h	hour	Pa	pascal
in	inch	psf	pounds per square foot
kg	kilogram	s	second
km	kilometre	sq ft	square foot
kN	kilonewton	WC	water closet

Glossary

This glossary of technical terms is intended to assist the general reader. *Words in italics denote a cross-reference.*

Barrel vault: A semi-cylindrical or partly cylindrical roof structure of constant cross section.

Bending moment: The *moment* due to the loads acting on the structure; the structure must be designed to resist the bending moment.

Beton: Concrete in French and German.

Buckling: Failure of compression member by deflection at right angles to the load.

Built-in: Rigidly restrained at the ends to prevent rotation.

Buttress: A projecting structure built against a wall to resist a horizontal force.

Came: Lead strip of H-section, used to hold pieces of glass in a window.

Cantilever: A projecting beam supported only at one end.

Cast iron: Iron with a carbon content between 1·8 and 4·5%, used as a structural material in the 18th and 19th centuries. It is weaker in tension and less ductile than *steel*.

Catenary: Curve assumed by a cable hanging under its own weight, *i.e.* the cable is purely in tension. A similar structure turned upside down forms a catenary arch which is purely in compression.

Centre of gravity: A body hanging from its centre of gravity is in equilibrium under its own weight.

Centroid: Synonym for *centre of gravity*.

Concrete: See: *plain concrete, precast concrete* and *prestressed concrete*.

Contraflexure, point of: The point where the curvature of a beam changes direction, *i.e.* where the slope changes from convex to concave. It can be shown that the *bending moment* is zero at a point of contraflexure.

Corbel: A piece of masonry projecting horizontally from the wall.

Creep: Deformation which occurs over a period of time without an increase in load.

Cross section: Section at right angles to the span.

Crown: The highest point of an arch, dome or vault.

Curtain wall: A thin external wall hung from a *skeleton frame*, as opposed to a loadbearing wall. The frame, not the wall, supports the roof and the floors.

Daylight factor: Ratio of illumination on a horizontal plane inside to the simultaneous exterior illumination.

Decibel: Unit for measuring sound levels.

Dial gauge: A mechanical device for measuring deflection which employs a train of gears to magnify the deflection.

Elastic deformation: Deformation fully recovered when the load is removed.

Electric resistance strain gauge: A very light electrical device for measuring *strains*, which can be glued to the structure; it utilises the change of resistance which occurs when the cross-sectional area of the wire is altered by straining.

Elevator: Synonym for lift.

Flat plate: In reinforced concrete construction, a concrete slab supported directly on the columns without enlarged column heads.

Flat slab: In reinforced concrete construction, a concrete slab supported on the columns through enlarged column heads, but without beams.

Flexure: Synonym for bending.

Flying buttress: A strut or half-arch which transmits the thrust of a vault or roof from the upper part of a wall to an outer *buttress* or support.

Formwork: Temporary structure used during construction, particularly for supporting wet concrete, to which it gives its form.

Golden section: A geometric construction for dividing a line into two unequal parts *a* and *b*, such that

$$b/a = \tfrac{1}{2}(1 + [5]^{\frac{1}{2}}) = 1\cdot618.$$

Great circle: The circles with the greatest diameter which can be drawn on a sphere; they correspond to straight lines on a plane surface. On the earth's surface the meridians of longitude and the equator are great circles. The remaining parallels of latitude are *small circles*.

Gypsum: Calcium sulphate dihydrate ($CaSO_4 \cdot 2H_2O$), a natural mineral which is the raw material for *plaster of Paris*; the Ancient Egyptians used gypsum as a mortar.

Hinge: A joint allowing free rotation.

Hooke's Law: Stress is proportional to *strain*.

Hoop force: Internal horizontal force in a dome, at right angles to the *meridional forces*.

Hoop tension: Tension which occurs in the lower portion of a hemispherical dome.

Hydraulic cement: A cement which is not washed out by water.

Hyperbolic paraboloid: A saddle-shaped surface which can be formed by two sets of straight lines.

Hypocaust: An underfloor heating system used by the Ancient Romans.

I-beam: A beam with two flanges, shaped like the letter I.

Jack arch: Short-span arch supporting a floor between closely spaced beams.

Keystone: The stone at the top of a masonry arch.

Lantern: Small open or glazed structure crowning a roof, particularly a dome.

Lever arm: Distance between the resultant tensile and compressive flexural forces in a cross section.

Lift: Synonym for elevator.

Lintel: A short-span beam, usually over a door or window opening.

Membrane structure: A structure free from bending.

Meridional force: Internal forces acting along the meridians of a dome, at right angles to the *hoop forces*.

Modulus of elasticity: Measure of *elastic deformation*, defined as the *stress* which would produce a unit *strain*. The modulus of elasticity in tension and compression is also called Young's modulus.

Moment: A force multiplied by the distance at which it acts.

Moment arm: Synonym for *lever arm*.

Moment distribution: A method for designing *statically indeterminate* structures (Section 3.8).

Moment of resistance: Internal moment in a beam which, for equilibrium, must equal the *bending moment* acting on the beam.

Mortise-and-tenon joint: Traditional timber joint formed by a mortise (rect-angular slot) into which the tenon (tongue) from another piece fits.

Nave: The body of a church, usually separated from the aisles by lines of pillars.

Neutral axis: Line at which the flexural stresses change from tension to compression.

Octagon: Eight-sided figure.

Pin joint: A joint allowing free rotation, whether formed by a pin or not.

Pinnacle: A vertical pointed structure rising above a roof or *buttress.*

Plain concrete: Concrete without reinforcement.

Plaster of Paris: Gypsum which has been heated to drive off some of its water ($CaSO_4 \cdot \frac{1}{2}H_2O$); it is used for plastering.

Plastic deformation: Deformation which is not recovered when the load is removed.

Plastic hinge: A pin joint formed by the *plastic deformation* of the material at high loads.

Plenum duct: A duct containing air under pressure slightly above that of its surroundings.

Point of contraflexure: See *contraflexure.*

Precast concrete: Concrete placed in position after casting, instead of being cast in place.

Prestressed concrete: Concrete which is precompressed in the zone where tensile stresses would normally occur under load, to eliminate those tensile stresses.

Reaction: Force exerted by the ground or by another structural member in opposition to the loads.

Resistance moment: See *moment of resistance.*

Rigid frame: A frame in which all or some of the joints are rigid, so that it becomes *statically indeterminate.*

Rigid joint: A joint which allows no rotation of the members joined relative to one another, that is, a right-angle joint remains a right-angle joint under load.

Shell: Thin curved structural surface.

Simply supported beam: A beam without restraints at the supports. It is *statically determinate.*

Skeleton frame: A frame which carries the *curtain walls.*

Slope-deflection analysis: A method for designing *statically indeterminate* structures (Section 3.8).

Small circle: A circle on the surface of a sphere smaller than a *great circle,* for example a parallel of latitude other than the equator.

Statically determinate: Soluble by statics alone.

Statically indeterminate: Insoluble by statics alone, because there are more members, *rigid joints* or *reactions* than there are statical equations.

Steel: An alloy of iron with a carbon content between 0.1 and 1.7%. Its structural properties are, on the whole, superior to both *cast iron* and *wrought iron.*

Strain: Deformation per unit length.

Strain energy: Energy stored up by *elastic deformation.* Strain energy methods can be used for the solution of statically indeterminate structures (Section 3.8).

Stress: Force per unit area.

Theorem of three moments: A theorem used for the solution of beams continuous over their supports.

Thrust: Compressive force or *reaction.*

Truss: An assembly of straight tension and compression members, which performs the same function as a deep beam.

Ultimate strength: The greatest strength of the structure, which is reached prior to its failure.

Wrought iron: Iron with a carbon content lower than *steel*, and consequently weaker. It was used as a structural material up to the 19th century.

Yield stress: The stress at which substantial *plastic deformation* first occurs.

Young's modulus: The *modulus of elasticity* in tension and compression.

Index